Don't Persuade, Pre-Suade!

By Daniel Melehi

©January 2024

Contents

Introduction

Welcome to the world of Pre-suasion, where the art of influence and persuasion is elevated to a whole new level. In this book, "Don't Persuade, Pre-suade!" we dive deep into the fascinating realm of pre-suasion and uncover the secrets to ethically shaping the thoughts, beliefs, and actions of others. In today's fast-paced and competitive world, the ability to persuade and influence others is a critical skill. Whether you are a marketer, salesperson, leader, or simply someone who wants to communicate effectively, understanding the principles and techniques of pre-suasion can give you that edge. Pre-suasion, coined by social psychologist Robert Cialdini, is the art of preparing the minds of your audience or target individuals for the message or request you want to convey. It involves creating favorable conditions and establishing the right context before presenting your argument or proposal. The power of pre-suasion lies in its ability to shape perception and prime the mind, increasing the likelihood of the desired outcome. By strategically framing a situation, leveraging psychological triggers, and utilizing various communication techniques, you can profoundly impact the decision-making process of others. Throughout this book, we explore the science behind pre-suasion, dissect its fundamental principles, and provide practical strategies and tactics for applying pre-suasion in various aspects of life. From marketing and sales to leadership and personal relationships, the concepts of pre-suasion can be utilized in almost every domain to achieve greater influence and desired outcomes. As we embark on this journey, we will delve into chapters that unravel the secrets of pre-suasion and equip you with the knowledge and tools to become a master influencer. We will explore the psychological underpinnings of pre-suasion, analyze the role of emotions and cognitive biases, and unveil how pre-suasion can be leveraged in different contexts. From crafting powerful pre-suasive messages to creating pre-suasive environments, we will cover it all. We will also showcase real-world case studies and success stories to illustrate the effectiveness of pre-suasion and inspire you to apply these principles in your own life. But it is essential to note that with great power comes great responsibility. In this book, we emphasize the importance of ethical pre-suasion and shield you from the pitfalls and mistakes that can undermine your efforts or harm others. So, get ready to harness the power of pre-suasion and unlock new possibilities in your personal and professional life. Let us begin this transformative journey into the art of pre-suasion, where small changes in perception can lead to significant changes in behavior.

THE POWER OF PRE-SUASION

In this chapter, we will explore the concept of pre-suasion and its profound influence on our decision-making process. Pre-suasion refers to the art of subtly shaping someone's perception or mindset before introducing a persuasive message or request. It is a strategic approach to influence that focuses on setting the stage for successful persuasion. Pre-suasion is based on the principle that people are more easily swayed when their attention and focus are redirected towards specific ideas or concepts. By strategically priming individuals with certain information or triggering certain emotions, it becomes more likely that they will be receptive to the persuasive message that follows. By understanding the power of pre-suasion, we can become more effective influencers and communicators. This chapter will delve into the various strategies and techniques that can be used to enhance pre-suasive impact and maximize the effectiveness of our persuasive efforts. We will explore the science behind pre-suasion, understanding how it works at a psychological level. By examining the cognitive biases and psychological triggers that influence decision-making, we can learn to leverage these principles in pre-suasive communication. Furthermore, we will discuss the importance of creating a pre-suasive mindset. This involves adopting a strategic approach to persuasion and understanding the key principles of pre-suasion. By cultivating a pre-suasive mindset, we can better align our goals with the psychological tendencies of our intended audience. Throughout this chapter, we will dive into the ways pre-suasion affects decision-making. We will explore the role of emotions in pre-suasion and how they can be utilized to create a receptive environment for persuasive messages. Additionally, we will examine the cognitive biases that influence decision-making and how we can leverage them in a pre-suasive manner. Ultimately, by mastering the strategies and techniques of pre-suasion, we can significantly increase the likelihood of achieving our persuasive objectives. This chapter will serve as a foundation for the subsequent chapters, where we will explore in-depth the application of pre-suasion in various contexts such as marketing, sales, leadership, personal relationships, politics, and more. So, buckle up and get ready to unleash the power of pre-suasion. By mastering this art, you will be equipped with a powerful tool to influence and persuade others effectively.

Chapter 2: Understanding the Pre-suasion Framework

In this chapter, we will dive deeper into the concept of pre-suasion and explore the framework that underlies its effectiveness. Understanding the pre-suasion framework is crucial for implementing persuasive strategies successfully. By comprehending the key elements and principles of pre-suasion, we can shape the way others perceive and respond to our messages.

THE FOUNDATION OF PRE-SUASION

At its core, pre-suasion is all about priming the recipient's mindset before presenting a persuasive message. It involves creating the right context and setting the stage for favorable reception. By redirecting attention towards specific ideas or emotions, we can influence decision-making in our desired direction. A crucial aspect of the pre-suasion framework is the concept of "anchoring." Anchoring refers to the phenomenon where the first piece of information encountered influences subsequent judgments and decisions. By strategically positioning an initial reference point or anchor, we can shape the recipient's perception and guide their thought process.

IDENTIFYING PRE-SUASIVE TRIGGERS

To effectively implement pre-suasion, it is essential to identify and utilize pre-suasive triggers. These triggers are elements that capture attention and direct focus towards specific ideas or emotions. They serve as psychological shortcuts that allow us to influence others more easily. One pre-suasive trigger is the concept of "perceived scarcity." People tend to value scarcity and rarity, and the fear of missing out can be a powerful motivator. By creating a sense of limited availability or urgency, we can tap into this trigger and increase the perceived value of our message or offer. Another pre-suasive trigger is "social proof." Humans have a tendency to conform to the actions or opinions of others, especially in uncertain situations. By showcasing testimonials, endorsements, or evidence of widespread adoption, we can leverage this trigger and influence others to align with our desired outcome.

THE ROLE OF CONTEXT IN PRE-SUASION

Context plays a crucial role in pre-suasion. The environment in which a persuasive message is delivered can significantly impact its effectiveness. By understanding the situational context, we can tailor our approach and increase the chances of achieving our desired outcome. For example, research has shown that positive moods or emotions can enhance the receptiveness to persuasive messages. By creating a positive and engaging environment, we can put the recipient in a more favorable mindset, increasing the likelihood of their agreement. Similarly, the physical setting and design can also influence pre-suasion. Strategic use of colors, visuals, and spatial arrangement can direct attention and shape perception. By designing the environment with pre-suasive elements in mind, we can enhance the impact of our message.

APPLYING THE PRE-SUASION FRAMEWORK

To effectively apply the pre-suasion framework, it is crucial to have a clear understanding of the desired outcome and the target audience. By aligning our pre-suasive strategies with the specific needs, preferences, and values of the audience, we can increase the effectiveness of our persuasive efforts. Additionally, it is important to consider ethical implications when utilizing pre-suasion. While pre-suasion can be a powerful tool for influencing others, it should always be used responsibly and with respect for the autonomy and well-being of individuals. By understanding the pre-suasion framework, identifying pre-suasive triggers, and considering the role of context, we can enhance our ability to persuade and influence others. In the following chapters, we will explore various techniques and strategies for effectively implementing pre-suasion in different scenarios and contexts.

Chapter 3: The Science behind Pre-suasion

Pre-suasion is not just a mere technique but a science that reveals the fascinating ways in which humans make decisions and form judgments. In this chapter, we will dive into the scientific principles that underpin the effectiveness of pre-suasion in influencing others. Understanding this science will empower you to become a more skilled and influential communicator.

THE PSYCHOLOGY OF PERSUASION

To comprehend the science behind pre-suasion, we need to explore the psychological factors that affect how individuals process information and make decisions. Several key principles play a crucial role in shaping human behavior and can be leveraged to achieve pre-suasive outcomes.

Priming

One central concept in the science of pre-suasion is priming. Priming refers to the process of presenting certain stimuli that subconsciously influence an individual's thoughts, perceptions, and subsequent behaviors. By introducing specific triggers, we can shape someone's mindset and predispose them to be more receptive to our persuasive message. For example, a study conducted by psychologists John Bargh and Mark Chen demonstrated that participants who were primed with words associated with the elderly, such as "Florida," "wrinkle," and "bingo," walked more slowly down a hallway compared to those who were not primed. This experiment shows how subtle cues can activate certain concepts and influence subsequent behavior.

Association and Linking

Another essential aspect of pre-suasion is the power of association. The human mind naturally creates links and connections between disparate ideas. By associating a specific concept or emotion with the message we want to convey, we can increase its persuasiveness. For instance, if you want to convince someone to support an environmental cause, showcasing images of idyllic landscapes, clean air, and happy children playing in nature can create a positive association. These associations can prime individuals to be more receptive to your persuasion and motivate them to take action.

NEUROSCIENCE AND PRE-SUASION

Advancements in neuroscience have provided valuable insights into how our brains respond to persuasive messages. Several brain regions play a crucial role in decision-making and can be targeted in pre-suasion strategies.

The Amygdala and Emotions

The amygdala, a key emotional center in the brain, plays a significant role in pre-suasion. Emotions strongly influence decision-making, and by activating specific emotions, we can shape how individuals evaluate information and form judgments. For example, if you want to convince someone to support a charitable cause, sharing a heartwarming story about the impact of their contribution can activate empathy in the listener. This emotional response can enhance their willingness to donate and support the cause.

The Prefrontal Cortex and Rational Thinking

In contrast to the emotional influence of the amygdala, the prefrontal cortex engages in rational thinking and decision-making. By presenting logical arguments and facts, we can activate the prefrontal cortex and appeal to the logical side of individuals. However, it's important to note that emotions still play a significant role even in rational decision-making. Emotions often influence our interpretation of facts and guide our choices. Therefore, a balanced approach that combines both emotional and logical appeals can be more persuasive.

APPLYING THE SCIENCE OF PRE-SUASION

Understanding the science behind pre-suasion equips us with a powerful toolset for effective communication and influence. By strategically leveraging the principles of priming, association, emotions, and rational thinking, we can shape the perception and decision-making of others. In the following chapters, we will explore specific techniques and strategies for implementing pre-suasion in various contexts, such as marketing, sales, leadership, and personal relationships. With a solid grasp of the science behind pre-suasion, you'll be able to craft compelling messages and create persuasive environments that increase the likelihood of achieving your desired outcomes.

KEY TAKEAWAYS

- Pre-suasion is rooted in the science of human behavior and decision-making. - Priming involves introducing specific stimuli that influence an individual's thoughts and subsequent behavior. - Association and linking concepts and emotions with our persuasive message increases its influence. - Understanding the influence of emotions and rational thinking in decision-making allows us to craft more effective pre-suasive messages. - Applying the science of pre-suasion empowers us to become more skilled communicators and influencers.

Chapter 4: Creating a Pre-suasive Mindset

In the previous chapters, we explored the power of pre-suasion and the science behind it. We learned how redirecting attention and leveraging cognitive biases can influence decision-making. Now, it's time to delve deeper into how to develop a pre-suasive mindset.

UNDERSTANDING THE MINDSET

To create a pre-suasive mindset, it's crucial to understand the underlying principles and strategies behind it. It goes beyond simply knowing the techniques; it requires a fundamental shift in how we approach persuasion. A pre-suasive mindset involves recognizing that persuasion is not just about the message itself, but about the context, timing, and framing surrounding it. It requires strategic thinking and a keen understanding of human psychology. It's about creating the right conditions to make people more receptive to our persuasive efforts.

STRATEGIC APPROACH TO PERSUASION

To develop a pre-suasive mindset, we need to adopt a strategic approach to persuasion. This involves careful planning and preparation before delivering a message, whether it's in a personal conversation, a business negotiation, or a marketing campaign. Firstly, we need to define our objectives and understand the desired outcome of our persuasive efforts. This clarity helps us focus our efforts and shape our message accordingly. Knowing what we want to achieve allows us to craft a more targeted and effective pre-suasive strategy. Next, we need to gather relevant information about our audience or target individuals. Understanding their needs, desires, and motivations enables us to tailor our message to resonate with them on a deeper level. By aligning our message with their values and aspirations, we increase the likelihood of capturing their attention and generating a positive response.

PERSISTENCE AND ADAPTABILITY

Developing a pre-suasive mindset also requires persistence and adaptability. It's important to recognize that not all attempts at persuasion will be successful, and that's okay. We need to be open to feedback and be willing to adjust our approach based on the results we observe. It's also crucial to be proactive and continuously seek opportunities for pre-suasive influence. This can involve creating environments that prime individuals for our message, building rapport and trust, or leveraging social influence.

THE POWER OF POSITIVE INFLUENCE

A pre-suasive mindset is not about manipulating or deceiving others. Instead, it focuses on understanding and positively influencing people's decision-making processes. It's about building trust, establishing credibility, and creating meaningful connections. When we approach persuasion with the intent to help and add value, rather than solely to benefit ourselves, we can develop a trusted and influential presence. By genuinely caring about the needs and desires of others, we increase our chances of successfully persuading them.

Key Takeaways

- Developing a pre-suasive mindset involves understanding the principles and strategies behind pre-suasion. - Strategy and preparation are key to effective persuasion. - Tailoring messages to align with the values and motivations of the target audience increases their receptiveness. - Persistence, adaptability, and a willingness to learn from feedback are important traits to develop. - Pre-suasion is a positive influence, focusing on building trust, credibility, and creating connections. By cultivating a pre-suasive mindset, we can become more impactful influencers and communicators, effectively shaping perceptions and guiding decision-making processes. The next chapters will explore how to apply this mindset in various contexts, from marketing and sales to personal relationships and leadership.

Chapter 5: How Pre-suasion Affects Decision Making

In this chapter, we will delve into the fascinating ways in which pre-suasion influences our decision-making processes. By understanding the underlying mechanisms at play, we can harness the power of pre-suasion to guide others towards making choices that align with our objectives.

THE INFLUENCE OF PRE-SUASION ON DECISION MAKING

Pre-suasion has a profound impact on decision making by priming individuals to focus on particular ideas, emotions, or considerations before they make a choice. By shaping their mindset before presenting a persuasive message or request, we increase the likelihood of success. One way pre-suasion affects decision making is by activating emotions. Emotions play a significant role in our decision-making processes, often guiding us instinctively towards certain choices. By strategically leveraging emotional triggers in pre-suasive communication, we can tap into deeply rooted feelings and encourage individuals to make decisions that are in line with our desired outcomes. Cognitive biases also come into play when pre-suading decision making. These biases are common patterns of thinking that can influence our judgments and choices. By understanding and leveraging these biases, we can subtly nudge individuals towards a specific decision. For example, the scarcity bias suggests that people tend to place more value on things that are scarce. By framing the options in a pre-suasive message in terms of limited availability, we can create a sense of urgency and increase the likelihood of a positive response.

THE ROLE OF ATTENTION IN DECISION MAKING

Attention is a crucial factor in decision making, and pre-suasion strategically directs attention towards specific aspects that are beneficial to our persuasive objectives. By capturing and redirecting attention towards certain information or ideas, we can shape the decision-making process in our favor. For example, imagine you are trying to persuade someone to invest in a new business venture. Instead of immediately presenting the facts and figures of the investment opportunity, you could begin the conversation by discussing the potential positive impact their investment could have on the community. By framing their attention towards the social benefits, you are pre-suading them to view the opportunity through a philanthropic lens, making it more likely for them to consider investing.

THE INFLUENCE OF FRAMING ON DECISION MAKING

Framing is a powerful pre-suasive technique that involves presenting information in a way that influences how it is perceived. By framing a message in a specific context, we can guide individuals towards making decisions that align with our goals. For example, a study conducted by researchers at Carnegie Mellon University found that framing a charity donation as an opportunity to gain social status and recognition increased the likelihood of individuals making a donation. By framing the act of donating as a way to enhance their social standing, the researchers leveraged a psychological trigger that influenced decision making in a pre-suasive manner.

CONCLUSION

Understanding how pre-suasion affects decision making enables us to become more effective influencers and communicators. By strategically utilizing emotions, cognitive biases, attention, and framing techniques, we can guide individuals towards making decisions that align with our objectives. In the next chapter, we will explore the role of emotions in pre-suasion and how they can be harnessed to create powerful persuasive messages.

Chapter 6: The Role of Emotions in Pre-suasion

Emotions are a powerful tool when it comes to influencing and persuading others. In this chapter, we will explore the role of emotions in pre-suasion and how they can be used strategically to shape perceptions and guide decision-making processes.

THE POWER OF EMOTIONAL APPEALS

Emotions play a significant role in our daily lives and greatly impact our decision-making processes. Research has shown that people often make decisions based on how they feel rather than relying solely on logic and reason. By understanding and leveraging this emotional drive, we can effectively pre-suade others. When it comes to persuasive communication, emotional appeals can be highly influential. Different emotions can elicit different responses, and by tapping into these emotional triggers, we can shape how individuals perceive and respond to our messages. For example, appealing to someone's sense of fear can prompt them to take action, while appealing to their desire for happiness and pleasure can motivate them to make a purchase.

THE ROLE OF PRIMING

In pre-suasion, priming is a powerful technique that involves exposing individuals to stimuli that activate specific emotions or associations before presenting a persuasive message. By priming individuals with certain emotions, we can set the stage for the desired response and increase the effectiveness of our persuasive efforts. Primed emotions can influence how information is processed and interpreted. When individuals are primed with positive emotions, they tend to be more open-minded and receptive to new ideas and suggestions. On the other hand, negative emotions can narrow their focus and make them more responsive to messages that offer solutions to their problems.

EMOTIONAL PERSUASIVE MESSAGES

Crafting effective emotional persuasive messages requires a deep understanding of the target audience's emotions, values, and motivations. By aligning our messages with these emotional drivers, we can create a stronger connection and increase the likelihood of persuasion. One effective strategy is to tell stories that evoke specific emotions in the audience. By sharing relatable narratives that tap into universal emotions such as happiness, sadness, or anger, we can create an emotional bond that fosters trust and empathy. Additionally, using vivid language and descriptive imagery can also help evoke emotional responses and make the persuasive message more impactful.

APPEALING TO THE POSITIVE AND NEGATIVE

It's important to acknowledge that emotions can be both positive and negative. While positive emotions such as joy and excitement can be powerful motivators, negative emotions such as fear and anxiety can also be used strategically to influence behavior. When appealing to positive emotions, highlight the benefits and rewards that individuals can experience as a result of taking the desired action. By painting a picture of a better future, you can create a sense of anticipation and enthusiasm. On the other hand, when appealing to negative emotions, identify and emphasize the potential problems or consequences that individuals may face if they don't take the desired action. By creating a sense of urgency and highlighting the potential loss, you can motivate individuals to act.

CONCLUSION

Emotions are a fundamental aspect of the human experience, and understanding their role in pre-suasion is crucial for effective persuasion. By leveraging emotional appeals, priming, and crafting persuasive messages that resonate with the target audience's emotions, we can create a strong connection and increase the likelihood of influencing their decisions. In the next chapter, we will delve into the fascinating world of cognitive biases and how they can be harnessed in pre-suasion to further enhance persuasive communication.

Chapter 7: Leveraging Cognitive Biases in Pre-suasion

In the realm of pre-suasion, understanding cognitive biases is a powerful tool for effectively influencing and persuading others. Cognitive biases are systematic patterns of deviation from rationality in judgment and decision-making. They are mental shortcuts that our brains rely on, often leading to biased thinking and decision-making processes. By leveraging these biases in pre-suasion, we can shape perceptions and guide individuals towards specific desired outcomes.

1. CONFIRMATION BIAS

Confirmation bias is the tendency to interpret information in a way that confirms one's preexisting beliefs or hypotheses. By targeting confirmation bias in pre-suasion, we can present information that aligns with the target audience's existing beliefs and values. This can create a sense of validation and reinforce their current perspectives, making them more receptive to our persuasive message.

2. ANCHORING BIAS

Anchoring bias occurs when individuals rely too heavily on the initial piece of information when making decisions. In pre-suasion, we can strategically provide an initial anchor that influences subsequent judgments and decisions. By presenting a favorable anchor or reference point, we can shape the perception of value or importance, increasing the likelihood of a desired outcome.

3. AVAILABILITY HEURISTIC

The availability heuristic is a mental shortcut where individuals make judgments based on the ease with which examples come to mind. In pre-suasion, we can strategically prime individuals with relevant examples or stories that evoke specific emotions and associations. By making these examples readily available in their minds, we can influence their decision-making process and steer it towards our desired outcome.

4. SOCIAL PROOF

Social proof bias refers to the tendency of individuals to conform to the actions or beliefs of others in a social group. In pre-suasion, we can leverage social proof by highlighting the actions or beliefs of influential individuals or groups who have already adopted our desired behavior or opinion. This can create a sense of social validation and encourage others to follow suit.

5. RECENCY BIAS

Recency bias occurs when individuals give greater weight to recent events or information when making judgments or decisions. In pre-suasion, we can strategically present the most compelling or persuasive information right before the moment of decision. By capitalizing on recency bias, we can increase the salience and impact of our persuasive message, making it more likely to sway individuals towards our desired outcome.

6. LOSS AVERSION

Loss aversion is the tendency of individuals to strongly prefer avoiding losses over acquiring gains. In pre-suasion, we can frame our persuasive message in terms of potential losses that individuals might incur if they do not adopt our desired behavior or opinion. By emphasizing the negative consequences of inaction, we can trigger loss aversion and motivate individuals to take the desired action.

7. AUTHORITY BIAS

Authority bias refers to the tendency of individuals to attribute greater credibility and trustworthiness to perceived authorities or experts. In pre-suasion, we can leverage authority bias by incorporating endorsements or testimonials from credible individuals or institutions. By aligning ourselves with authoritative figures, we can enhance our persuasive message's perceived credibility and influence. By understanding and leveraging these cognitive biases in pre-suasion, we can tailor our messages and tactics to align with the quirks of human decision-making processes. However, it is essential to approach these techniques ethically and responsibly, ensuring that pre-suasion is used to facilitate positive influence and not to manipulate or deceive others. In the next chapter, we will explore the concept of social influence in pre-suasion and its impact on persuasive communication.

Chapter 8: Utilizing Social Influence in Pre-suasion

Social influence plays a significant role in shaping our perceptions and decisions. As social creatures, we tend to look to others for guidance on how to think, feel, and behave. Understanding and leveraging social influence can be a powerful tool in pre-suasion and persuasion.

SOCIAL PROOF: THE POWER OF CONFORMITY

One of the most potent forms of social influence is social proof. Social proof is the tendency to conform to the actions or beliefs of others, especially when we are unsure or in unfamiliar situations. By providing evidence that others have already taken a specific action or hold a particular belief, we can influence individuals to follow suit. In the context of pre-suasion, utilizing social proof involves showcasing the behavior or opinions of others as a means to persuade. This can be done through testimonials, reviews, or case studies that demonstrate how others have benefited from the desired action or belief. By highlighting the social consensus surrounding a particular idea or behavior, we tap into the innate human desire to fit in and be part of a group.

AUTHORITY: THE INFLUENCE OF CREDIBLE SOURCES

Another crucial aspect of social influence is authority. People tend to trust and respect individuals or institutions that are perceived as credible and knowledgeable in a specific domain. Incorporating endorsements or testimonials from authoritative figures can significantly enhance the credibility and persuasiveness of a message. In pre-suasion, utilizing authority involves associating the desired action or belief with respected and influential individuals or institutions. This can be achieved through celebrity endorsements, expert opinions, or references to well-established organizations. By aligning the desired behavior or attitude with credible sources, we tap into the underlying psychological mechanism of trust, making it more likely that individuals will be persuaded to act in a desired way.

CONSISTENCY: THE DRIVE FOR ALIGNMENT

Humans have a natural inclination to behave in ways that are consistent with their previous actions, values, and commitments. This drive for alignment stems from our desire to maintain a positive self-image and avoid cognitive dissonance. Leveraging consistency in pre-suasion involves emphasizing the alignment between the desired action or belief and an individual's existing attitudes or values. To utilize consistency, it is essential to identify and highlight the common ground between the target audience's current mindset and the desired outcome. By framing the persuasive message in a way that aligns with their existing beliefs or values, we create a sense of internal consistency. This alignment increases the likelihood that individuals will be receptive to the persuasive message and more willing to take the desired action.

CONCLUSION

Utilizing social influence in pre-suasion is a powerful strategy for increasing persuasion effectiveness. By leveraging social proof, authority, and consistency, we can tap into the innate human tendency to conform, trust credible sources, and maintain alignment. Understanding and employing these social influence techniques can significantly enhance the persuasiveness of our messages and increase the likelihood of achieving desired outcomes.

In the next chapter, we will explore the art of crafting powerful pre-suasive messages.

Chapter 9: Crafting Powerful Pre-suasive Messages

In the previous chapters, we explored the power of pre-suasion, the science behind it, and how it influences decision-making. Now, let's dive into the art of crafting powerful pre-suasive messages. Crafting a pre-suasive message requires careful consideration of the target audience, their values, motivations, and emotions. It's about designing messages that resonate with them on a deep level, capturing their attention and influencing their perception before even presenting the persuasive content. Here are some strategies to help you craft powerful pre-suasive messages:

1. UNDERSTAND YOUR TARGET AUDIENCE

To create a pre-suasive message that resonates with your audience, you need to fully understand who they are, what they care about, and what motivates them. Conduct market research, gather data, and analyze your target audience's demographics, psychographics, and behavioral patterns. This information will enable you to tailor your message to their specific needs and desires.

2. USE EMOTIONAL APPEAL

Emotions have a profound impact on decision-making, and tapping into them can make your pre-suasive message more impactful. Identify the emotions that are relevant to your audience and craft your message in a way that elicits those emotions. Whether it's joy, fear, anger, or empathy, triggering the right emotions can establish a strong connection and motivate action.

3. CREATE A COMPELLING NARRATIVE

Storytelling is a powerful tool in pre-suasion. Create a narrative that engages your audience and takes them on a journey. Use vivid language, relatable characters, and compelling anecdotes to evoke emotions and capture their attention. A well-crafted story can make your message more memorable and persuasive.

4. PROVIDE SOCIAL PROOF

People tend to follow the actions and beliefs of others, especially those they perceive as influential or similar to themselves. Incorporating social proof in your message can increase its pre-suasive impact. Use testimonials, case studies, or endorsements from satisfied customers or respected authorities to build trust and credibility.

5. HIGHLIGHT BENEFITS AND REWARDS

Focus on the benefits and rewards that your product, service, or idea offers. Clearly communicate how it can improve the lives of your audience and meet their needs or desires. Highlight the positive outcomes they can expect by taking the desired action. This positive framing can create a sense of anticipation and motivation.

6. ADDRESS POTENTIAL CONCERNS

Anticipate and address potential concerns or objections that your audience may have. By acknowledging and overcoming their doubts or hesitations, you can alleviate their worries and increase their likelihood of being influenced by your message. Be transparent, provide evidence, or offer solutions to any potential barriers.

7. KEEP IT SIMPLE AND CLEAR

Avoid overwhelming your audience with complex or convoluted messaging. Keep your pre-suasive messages simple, clear, and easy to understand. Use concise and straightforward language that everyone can grasp. Providing clear instructions or a call to action ensures that the audience knows exactly what you want them to do and how to do it.

8. TEST AND ITERATE

Crafting powerful pre-suasive messages is an iterative process. Continuously test different variations of your messages to gauge their effectiveness. Conduct A/B tests, collect feedback, and analyze the results. Refine and optimize your messages based on the insights you gather to improve their pre-suasive impact. Remember, crafting powerful pre-suasive messages is an art that requires a deep understanding of your audience, strategic storytelling, and effective use of emotions and social influence. By implementing these strategies, you can shape perceptions, capture attention, and increase the likelihood of achieving your pre-suasive objectives. Next, we'll explore how to captivate attention and build interest in Chapter 10: Captivating Attention and Building Interest.

Chapter 10: Captivating Attention and Building Interest

In the world of persuasion, capturing attention is the first step towards influencing others. Without drawing someone's focus, it becomes nearly impossible to communicate your message effectively. Additionally, building interest is crucial for keeping individuals engaged and receptive to your persuasive efforts. In this chapter, we will explore strategies and techniques for captivating attention and building interest in pre-suasion.

THE POWER OF ATTENTION

Attention is a limited resource in today's fast-paced, information-overloaded world. People are constantly bombarded with stimuli, making it challenging to capture and hold their focus. To make matters more difficult, attention spans have become increasingly shorter, making it even more vital to stand out from the noise. To captivate attention, it's important to understand what grabs people's interest. Novelty is a key factor - presenting something new or unexpected is more likely to pique curiosity and capture attention. You can achieve this by offering unique insights, presenting counterintuitive information, or even using surprising visuals or storytelling techniques. Another effective way to capture attention is by tapping into emotions. Emotions are powerful drivers of attention, and evoking curiosity, excitement, or intrigue can significantly increase engagement. For example, you might start with a thought-provoking question or introduce a vivid and compelling anecdote that immediately hooks your audience.

BUILDING INTEREST

Once you have managed to capture attention, the next step is to build and maintain interest throughout your persuasion efforts. Interest acts as a fuel that keeps individuals engaged and receptive to your message, making them more likely to be influenced by your ideas. One effective strategy for building interest is by aligning your message with the interests and values of your audience. When people feel that your message is personally relevant and valuable to them, they are more likely to pay attention and engage with what you have to say. By understanding your audience's needs, desires, and motivations, you can tailor your message to resonate deeply with them. Additionally, storytelling can be a powerful tool for building interest. Humans are naturally drawn to narratives, and well-crafted stories can captivate attention and create emotional connections. Consider incorporating relevant and compelling stories or case studies that illustrate the benefits or consequences of your persuasive message. This will not only grab attention but also make your message more memorable and impactful. It's important to note that maintaining interest requires a balance between novelty and familiarity. While novelty initially captures attention, it can quickly wear off if there is no sustained interest. Therefore, it's crucial to provide new and valuable information while also reinforcing familiar concepts or ideas that your audience can connect with.

STRATEGIES FOR CAPTIVATING ATTENTION AND BUILDING INTEREST

Here are some practical strategies for captivating attention and building interest in your pre-suasion efforts:

1. Start with a bang:

Open your message with a compelling statement, thought-provoking question, or intriguing anecdote that immediately grabs attention and generates curiosity.

2. Utilize visual stimuli:

Incorporate visually captivating elements such as images, infographics, or videos to engage the visual senses and create a powerful impact.

3. Evoke emotions:

Appeal to the emotions of your audience by incorporating stories, personal experiences, or relatable examples that elicit curiosity, excitement, or empathy.

4. Use conversational language:

Communicate in a conversational and relatable tone to establish a connection with your audience and make your message more engaging.

5. Provide unique insights:

Offer fresh perspectives, unique data, or surprising facts that challenge conventional thinking and ignite curiosity.

6. Highlight benefits and outcomes:

Clearly communicate the benefits and outcomes that your audience can expect from embracing your persuasive message. This helps build interest by showing the value of your proposition.

7. Create suspense:

Craft your message in a way that leaves some information or details to be revealed later, building anticipation and keeping your audience hooked.

8. Use interactive elements:

Incorporate interactive elements such as polls, quizzes, or interactive presentations to actively engage your audience and keep their interest alive. By implementing these strategies, you can effectively captivate attention and build interest in your pre-suasion efforts. Remember, the more engaged and interested your audience is, the higher the chances of successfully influencing their thoughts and behaviors. Next, we will explore the importance of establishing trust and credibility in pre-suasion.

Chapter 11: Establishing Trust and Credibility

Building trust and establishing credibility are crucial elements in effectively persuading and influencing others. Without trust, your message may fall on deaf ears, and your efforts to persuade may be in vain. In this chapter, we will explore strategies and techniques for establishing trust and credibility in pre-suasion.

THE IMPORTANCE OF TRUST AND CREDIBILITY

Trust is the foundation of any successful relationship, whether personal or professional. It is the belief that someone is reliable, honest, and competent. Establishing trust is essential because people are more likely to be open to your persuasive message if they trust you. Credibility is closely related to trust. It refers to the perception of your expertise, knowledge, and authority in a particular subject matter. When you are seen as credible, people are more likely to believe what you say and follow your suggestions. When aiming to be persuasive, trust and credibility serve as the pillars that support your message. Without them, your efforts may be met with skepticism or resistance. Therefore, it is essential to focus on establishing trust and credibility from the outset.

BUILDING TRUST

To establish trust, consider the following strategies:

1. Be Honest and Transparent

Openness and honesty are crucial for building trust. Be transparent about your intentions and motives. Avoid exaggerations or false claims. People appreciate honesty and are more likely to trust someone who is genuine.

2. Demonstrate Competence

One of the key factors that contribute to trustworthiness is competence. Show expertise in your field by showcasing your knowledge and experience. Provide relevant evidence, such as certifications, case studies, or success stories, to demonstrate your competence.

3. Maintain Consistency

Consistency breeds trust. Consistently deliver on your promises, meet deadlines, and follow through on your commitments. Demonstrating reliability and consistency will help build trust over time.

4. Show Empathy and Understanding

Empathy is an essential element in building trust. Show genuine care and understanding towards others' needs and concerns. Listen actively, acknowledge their feelings, and validate their perspectives. By demonstrating empathy, you create a sense of trust and rapport.

Establishing Credibility

In addition to building trust, establishing credibility is equally significant for effective persuasion. Consider the following strategies to enhance your credibility:

1. Leverage Social Proof

Social proof is a powerful tool for building credibility. Highlight positive feedback, testimonials, or endorsements from satisfied customers or well-known individuals in your field. When others see that respected individuals or organizations endorse you, they are more likely to perceive you as credible.

2. Demonstrate Expertise

Position yourself as an expert by sharing valuable insights and knowledge in your field. Write informative articles, give presentations, or participate in industry-related events. Establishing yourself as an authority figure will increase your credibility.

3. Provide Evidence and Data

Back up your claims with credible evidence and data. Use research studies, statistics, or case studies to support your arguments. Providing concrete evidence adds credibility to your message and enhances your persuasive impact.

4. Establish Your Online Presence

In today's digital age, having a strong online presence can significantly contribute to your credibility. Maintain an up-to-date website or blog, engage with your audience on social media platforms, and share valuable content. Building a reputable online presence will help establish your credibility. By combining trust-building strategies with credibility-enhancing techniques, you can maximize your persuasive potential. Remember, establishing trust and credibility is an ongoing process. It requires consistency, sincerity, and continuous effort. The more trust and credibility you build, the more persuasive and influential you become. In the next chapter, we will explore the concept of tapping into the power of authority in pre-suasion.

Chapter 12: Tapping into the Power of Authority

Authority holds a powerful influence over our decision-making processes. When we perceive someone as an authority figure, we are more likely to trust their opinions and follow their guidance. Understanding and leveraging the power of authority can significantly enhance our ability to persuade and influence others.

THE IMPORTANCE OF AUTHORITY

Authority is a psychological concept that shapes our perception of credibility and expertise. It is deeply ingrained in human behavior and manifests in various forms, such as titles, credentials, and positions of power. When individuals perceive someone as possessing authority, they are more likely to comply with their requests or suggestions. In the context of persuasion, tapping into the power of authority can be a highly effective strategy. By positioning ourselves or others as authorities, we can increase our persuasive influence and sway others to adopt our viewpoints or take desired actions.

LEVERAGING AUTHORITY IN PRE-SUASION

To tap into the power of authority in pre-suasion, it is crucial to establish and reinforce credibility. Here are some strategies to consider:

1. Highlight Relevant Expertise

When attempting to persuade others, it is essential to showcase your or others' expertise in the relevant domain. Highlighting relevant experience, qualifications, and achievements helps establish credibility and signals to others that you have the necessary knowledge and competence to offer valuable insights or recommendations.

2. Incorporate Endorsements and Testimonials

Endorsements and testimonials from credible individuals or reputable institutions can significantly enhance persuasive messages. When others see that respected authorities endorse a product, service, or idea, they are more likely to trust and accept it as well. Including quotes or statements from recognized experts or trusted sources can add credibility to your pre-suasive communication.

3. Reference Consensus from Expert Communities

When there is a consensus among experts within a particular field, referencing this agreement can strengthen your pre-suasive message. People are more likely to align with the opinions or recommendations of a community of experts rather than an individual authority figure alone. Utilizing consensus from reputable expert communities can enhance the perceived authority of your message.

4. Emphasize Credentials and Titles

Credentials and titles can play a significant role in establishing authority. Incorporating relevant credentials and titles when introducing yourself or others can enhance credibility and influence. However, it is crucial to ensure that the credentials and titles are genuinely relevant and respected within the context you are addressing. Misusing or overstating credentials can undermine your credibility.

5. Maintain Confidence and Poise

Confidence and poise are essential attributes of authoritative individuals. When presenting your persuasive message, it is vital to exhibit confidence without appearing arrogant. The way you carry yourself and articulate your points can significantly impact the perception of your authority. Set the tone by projecting confidence and maintaining a composed demeanor throughout your communication.

ETHICAL CONSIDERATIONS

While leveraging authority can be influential, it is important to use this power responsibly and ethically. Manipulating or fabricating authority can lead to distrust and damage relationships. Therefore, it is crucial to ensure that the authority presented is genuine and aligned with the expertise or credentials being claimed.

SUMMARY

Tapping into the power of authority is a crucial aspect of pre-suasion. By establishing credibility and leveraging relevant expertise, endorsements, and titles, we can enhance our persuasive influence. However, it is essential to use authority ethically and responsibly to maintain trust and credibility. Understanding and harnessing the power of authority strengthens our ability to guide others' perceptions and influence their decision-making processes. Next, we will explore how likability plays a role in pre-suasion and how to cultivate positive connections with our audience.

Chapter 13: Harnessing the Principles of Likability

When it comes to persuasion, likability plays a crucial role in influencing others. People are more likely to be persuaded by someone they like and trust. Harnessing the principles of likability can significantly enhance your persuasive abilities.

THE POWER OF LIKABILITY

Likability refers to the degree to which others find you pleasant, appealing, and enjoyable to be around. When someone likes you, they are more likely to listen to your message, trust your recommendations, and be open to persuasion. Likability is a fundamental aspect of social influence. Research has shown that people are more likely to comply with requests and suggestions from individuals they perceive as likable. Likable individuals also enjoy more positive interactions and relationships, which can greatly benefit their persuasion efforts.

BUILDING LIKABILITY

Building likability involves creating rapport and connection with others. Here are some strategies to harness the principles of likability and increase your persuasive effectiveness:

1. Establish common ground:

Find shared interests, experiences, or values with your audience. When people feel a connection with you, they are more likely to trust and listen to what you have to say.

2. Show empathy and understanding:

Demonstrate that you genuinely care about your audience's needs, concerns, and problems. By showing understanding and empathy, you build trust and establish a stronger connection.

3. Use positive body language:

Nonverbal cues such as smiling, maintaining eye contact, and open body posture can make you more approachable and likable. Pay attention to your body language to ensure you come across as warm and friendly.

4. Be genuine and authentic:

People appreciate authenticity and can quickly sense when someone is being fake or insincere. Be yourself and let your true personality shine through in your interactions.

5. Demonstrate active listening:

Ensure that you are fully present and attentive when engaging with your audience. Listen actively, ask relevant questions, and provide thoughtful responses. This shows that you value their input and perspectives.

6. Provide value:

Offer something of value to your audience, whether it's useful information, insights, or assistance. When people perceive you as helpful and knowledgeable, they are more likely to view you favorably and be influenced by your message.

7. Use humor:

Humor can be a powerful tool for building likability. Sharing a well-timed, appropriate joke or amusing anecdote can help establish a positive emotional connection and make you more relatable.

APPLYING LIKABILITY IN PERSUASION

Once you have established likability, you can apply it strategically in your persuasive efforts. Here are some ways to do so:

1. Align your message with your audience's values:

When crafting your persuasive message, consider the values and beliefs of your audience. Highlight how your proposal aligns with their values, making them more likely to be receptive to your ideas.

2. Use social proof:

Leverage likability by showcasing endorsements or testimonials from likable individuals who support your message. People are more likely to trust and follow the actions of those they perceive as likable.

3. Create positive emotional associations:

Use positive emotional appeals in your message to build likability and make your ideas more appealing. Tell stories, use uplifting language, and evoke positive emotions that resonate with your audience.

4. Collaborate rather than coerce:

Approach persuasion as a collaborative process rather than a one-sided attempt to force compliance. Engage your audience in discussions, seek their input, and make them feel like valued contributors.

5. Maintain a positive attitude:

Positivity is contagious. By maintaining a positive attitude during the persuasion process, you can create a positive and enjoyable experience for your audience. This can enhance likability and increase their receptiveness to your message.

CONCLUSION

Harnessing the principles of likability is a powerful strategy for enhancing persuasion. By building rapport, demonstrating empathy, and using positive body language, you can establish likability and increase your persuasive effectiveness. Applying likability in persuasion involves aligning your message with your audience's values, using social proof, creating positive emotional associations, collaborating rather than coercing, and maintaining a positive attitude. By mastering the principles of likability, you can become a more influential and persuasive communicator.

Chapter 14: Creating Scarcity and Urgency

In the world of persuasion and influence, scarcity and urgency are powerful psychological triggers that can significantly impact decision-making processes. When something is limited in availability or time-sensitive, people tend to perceive it as more valuable and desirable. As a result, they may feel a sense of urgency to act quickly or fear missing out on a great opportunity.

THE POWER OF SCARCITY

Scarcity is the perception that a resource or opportunity is limited or rare. When something is scarce, it taps into the fear of missing out (FOMO) and triggers a sense of urgency in individuals. Marketers and persuaders have long understood the power of scarcity and have used it to influence behavior in various contexts. One common way to create scarcity is by highlighting limited quantities. For example, a retail store might advertise a sale with a statement like, "Only 10 left in stock!" By implying that the product is selling fast and might run out soon, the store creates a sense of scarcity and drives individuals to make a purchase. Another effective technique is time-based scarcity. This involves setting deadlines or time limits for an offer or opportunity. For instance, a limited-time discount or a flash sale that lasts only a few hours can create a sense of urgency and push individuals to take immediate action.

THE ROLE OF URGENCY

Urgency complements scarcity by adding an element of immediacy to the persuasive message. It creates a sense of pressure in individuals and makes them feel compelled to act quickly. Urgency taps into the human tendency to prioritize time-sensitive matters over those that can be delayed or postponed. One way to create urgency is by presenting a time-limited offer. For instance, a clothing store might advertise a sale with a clear end date, such as "Sale ends tomorrow!" By setting a deadline, the store triggers a sense of urgency and encourages individuals to make a purchase before it's too late. Another strategy is to use scarcity and urgency together. For example, a hotel booking website might display a message like, "Only 3 rooms available at this price! Book now before they're gone!" By combining both scarcity and urgency, the website incites individuals to take immediate action to secure the limited available rooms.

THE PSYCHOLOGICAL PRINCIPLES BEHIND SCARCITY AND URGENCY

Scarcity and urgency tap into various psychological principles that influence decision making. One such principle is the fear of missing out (FOMO), which is the anxiety that arises from the possibility of not experiencing something desirable or valuable. By creating a sense of scarcity or urgency, persuaders can exploit this fear and drive individuals to take action. Another principle at play is loss aversion, which is the tendency to strongly prefer avoiding losses over acquiring equivalent gains. Scarcity and urgency trigger a fear of potential loss, as individuals risk missing out on an opportunity or losing access to a limited resource. This fear can be a powerful motivator that compels individuals to act quickly before it's too late. Additionally, scarcity and urgency appeal to the basic human desire for exclusivity and uniqueness. When something is scarce or time-sensitive, it becomes more desirable because it is perceived as rare and valuable. People often want what they can't easily obtain, and scarcity and urgency create a sense of exclusivity that increases the perceived value of the offer or opportunity.

APPLYING SCARCITY AND URGENCY ETHICALLY

While scarcity and urgency can be powerful tools for persuasion, it's important to use them ethically and responsibly. Creating artificial scarcity or using false urgency tactics can erode trust and credibility, damaging long-term relationships with customers or individuals. To apply scarcity and urgency ethically, it's important to ensure that the scarcity is genuine and the urgency is legitimate. Communicate transparently and truthfully about the availability or time constraints of the offer or opportunity. Avoid using manipulative tactics that deceive or coerce individuals into making decisions they might later regret. Additionally, it's crucial to provide clear and concise information about the benefits or value of the offer or opportunity. Scarcity and urgency should enhance the perceived value rather than being the sole basis for decision-making.

STRATEGIES FOR CREATING SCARCITY AND URGENCY

1. Limited availability: Highlight the limited quantities or stock of a product or service to create a sense of scarcity. 2. Time-limited offers: Set clear deadlines or time limits for an offer or opportunity to create a sense of urgency. 3. Countdowns and timers: Use visual cues like countdowns or timers to visually represent the limited time available. 4. Exclusive access: Offer early access or VIP privileges to a

select group of individuals, creating a sense of exclusivity and scarcity. 5. Limited editions or releases: Create special editions or limited releases of products or services, emphasizing their exclusivity and rarity. 6. Special bonuses or incentives: Offer additional perks or bonuses for a limited time to incentivize immediate action. 7. Social proof: Highlight the increasing popularity or demand for the product or service to create a sense of scarcity and urgency. Remember, the goal should always be to provide value and meet the needs and desires of your audience. Scarcity and urgency can be effective tools when used responsibly and ethically to enhance the persuasive message and influence decision-making processes.

Chapter 15: The Art of Setting the Stage for Pre-suasion

In the realm of persuasion, setting the stage is just as important as delivering the message itself. The art of setting the stage for pre-suasion involves creating an environment that primes individuals to be more receptive to your persuasive message. By setting the right context, you can enhance the effectiveness of your pre-suasive techniques and increase the likelihood of influencing others.

UNDERSTANDING THE IMPACT OF ENVIRONMENT

Our surroundings and the context in which communication takes place can significantly influence our thoughts, emotions, and behaviors. Whether we realize it or not, we are constantly being influenced by our environment. By understanding the impact of the environment on decision-making processes, we can strategically design settings that align with our persuasive objectives. One key aspect of setting the stage for pre-suasion is the physical environment. The layout, colors, lighting, and overall aesthetics can shape individuals' perceptions and create a specific mood or atmosphere. For example, a brightly lit room with warm colors can evoke positive emotions and a sense of comfort, making individuals more receptive to persuasive messages. Additionally, the social environment plays a crucial role in pre-suasion. People are heavily influenced by the actions and beliefs of those around them. By leveraging social norms and peer pressure, you can create an environment that encourages conformity and aligns individuals' behaviors with your persuasive goals. For example, highlighting the popularity and widespread acceptance of a particular idea or product can motivate individuals to adopt the same beliefs or behaviors.

DESIGNING PERSUASIVE ENVIRONMENTS

When it comes to setting the stage for pre-suasion, careful attention should be given to the design of the environment. Here are some strategies for designing persuasive environments:

1. Contextual cues:

Consider the broader context in which the communication will take place. Are there any specific cues or symbols that can be incorporated to prime individuals' thoughts and emotions? For example, if you're trying to persuade individuals to adopt a healthier lifestyle, incorporating images of fit and active individuals can serve as powerful contextual cues.

2. Framing:

Frame the environment in a way that aligns with your persuasive message. Use language, visuals, and symbols that reinforce the desired beliefs or behaviors. For example, if you're promoting environmentally friendly products, using recycled materials in the physical environment can reinforce the message of sustainability.

3. Environmental triggers:

Identify specific triggers or stimuli that can activate desired thoughts, emotions, or associations. For example, playing soothing music in a waiting room can create a calming atmosphere and reduce anxiety, making individuals more receptive to your message.

4. Personalization:

Tailor the environment to the individual preferences and characteristics of your target audience. Consider their cultural background, age group, and values when designing the environment. This personal touch can create a sense of familiarity and connection, enhancing the effectiveness of your persuasive efforts.

5. Consistency:

Ensure that the environment is consistent with the message you're conveying. Any inconsistencies can create cognitive dissonance and reduce the persuasive impact. For example, if you're promoting a high-end luxury product, the environment should reflect a sense of exclusivity and sophistication.

MEASURING THE IMPACT

Setting the stage for pre-suasion is not a one-size-fits-all approach. It requires careful planning, implementation, and evaluation. Measuring the impact of the environment on persuasion can help identify areas of improvement and optimize future efforts. One way to measure the impact is through observation and feedback. Monitor individuals' behaviors, reactions, and engagement levels in the persuasive environment. Collect feedback through surveys or interviews to gain insights into their perceptions and experiences. Additionally, conducting A/B testing can provide valuable data on the effectiveness of different environmental designs. Create multiple versions of the environment and test them with different groups to identify the most impactful elements.

CONCLUSION

Setting the stage for pre-suasion is a powerful tool for enhancing the effectiveness of persuasive communication. By creating environments that align with your persuasive goals, you can significantly increase the likelihood of influencing others. Understanding the impact of the environment, strategically designing persuasive environments, and measuring their impact are key steps in mastering the art of setting the stage for pre-suasion.

Chapter 16: Designing Pre-suasive Environments

The environment in which communication takes place plays a significant role in shaping perceptions, emotions, and behaviors. By strategically designing pre-suasive environments, we can enhance the effectiveness of our persuasive messages and increase the likelihood of influencing others.

THE IMPACT OF THE PHYSICAL ENVIRONMENT

The physical environment, including factors such as layout, colors, lighting, and ambient noise, can significantly influence how individuals perceive and process information. When designing a pre-suasive environment, consider the following strategies:

1. Contextual Cues

Carefully select and arrange elements in the environment to provide cues that align with the desired message. For example, if you're trying to persuade someone to adopt a healthier lifestyle, surround them with images of active and fit individuals. These visual cues act as reminders and prime their mindset towards healthier choices.

2. Framing

Frame the physical environment in a way that directs attention towards the desired message. For instance, if you're promoting a new product, strategically place it in an area that attracts attention and encourages exploration. Use signage and displays to highlight its unique features and benefits.

3. Environmental Triggers

Introduce elements that evoke specific emotions or associations related to the persuasive message. Use scents, music, or ambient sound to create an emotional atmosphere that aligns with your objectives. For example, if you're promoting a relaxing spa experience, play soft music and diffuse calming scents to create a tranquil environment.

4. Personalization

Customize the environment to individual preferences whenever possible. Personalization enhances engagement and makes individuals feel more connected to the message. For example, if you're hosting a conference, ask attendees about their dietary preferences and provide customized meal options.

5. Consistency

Ensure that the physical environment aligns with the message you're conveying. Consistency creates a sense of coherence and reinforces the intended messaging. For example, if you're promoting a sustainable lifestyle, use eco-friendly materials and incorporate natural elements into the environment.

MEASURING THE IMPACT OF PRE-SUASIVE ENVIRONMENTS

To gauge the effectiveness of your pre-suasive environment, it's important to gather feedback and observe individuals' responses. Consider implementing A/B testing by creating two different environments and comparing their impact on individuals' attitudes and behaviors. Additionally, encourage individuals to provide feedback on their experiences and use that information to inform future improvements.

1. Observation

Observe how individuals interact with and respond to the pre-suasive environment. Pay attention to their body language, level of engagement, and any changes in behavior. Are they more receptive to the message? Are they more likely to engage in the desired action? These observations can provide valuable insights into the effectiveness of your design.

2. Feedback

Encourage individuals to provide feedback on their experience in the pre-suasive environment. Use surveys or interviews to gather their thoughts, feelings, and perceptions. Ask specific questions about the environmental elements that stood out to them and how those elements influenced their decision-making process.

3. A/B Testing

Implementing A/B testing involves creating two different pre-suasive environments and randomly assigning individuals to experience one of them. Compare the responses and behaviors of individuals in each environment to determine which design is more effective in achieving your persuasive objectives. Iterate and refine your designs based on the findings.

SUMMARY

Designing pre-suasive environments involves strategically shaping the physical environment to enhance the effectiveness of persuasive messages. By considering factors such as contextual cues, framing, environmental triggers, personalization, and consistency, we can create environments that prime individuals for the desired response. Measuring the impact through observation, feedback, and A/B testing helps us refine and optimize our designs for maximum influence. In the next chapter, we will explore the role of nonverbal communication in pre-suasion.

Chapter 17: Mastering Nonverbal Communication in Pre-suasion

Nonverbal communication plays a crucial role in pre-suasion. It encompasses all the messages we convey without using words, including facial expressions, body language, gestures, vocal tone, and personal appearance. Mastering nonverbal communication in pre-suasion can significantly impact the effectiveness of persuasive messages.

THE POWER OF NONVERBAL CUES

Nonverbal cues can amplify or contradict the verbal message being delivered, making them a valuable tool in pre-suasion. They can shape perceptions, build trust, and influence decision-making. Here are a few key nonverbal cues to consider:

1. Facial Expressions:

Facial expressions can communicate emotions, trustworthiness, and sincerity. Smiling, for example, can create a positive and approachable impression. It is essential to align your facial expressions with the message you want to convey.

2. Body Language:

Body language includes gestures, posture, and movement. Adopting an open and relaxed posture can signal approachability and confidence. Maintaining eye contact shows attentiveness and engagement. Matching your body language to the desired outcome can enhance pre-suasion.

3. Vocal Tone and Delivery:

The tone of voice and the way you deliver your message can greatly impact how it is received. Speaking confidently, with appropriate variation in pitch and intonation, can convey credibility and influence others' emotions. Pay attention to your tone and delivery to align with your pre-suasive goals.

4. Personal Appearance:

Your personal appearance contributes to the overall impression you make. Dressing appropriately for the context and projecting a professional image can enhance your credibility and influence. Consider how your appearance aligns with the message you are trying to convey.

NONVERBAL COMMUNICATION IN PRE-SUASION STRATEGIES

When applying nonverbal communication in pre-suasion, it's crucial to consider context, audience, and desired outcomes. Here are some strategies to master nonverbal communication for maximum persuasive impact:

1. Mirror and Match:

Mirroring and matching the nonverbal cues of your audience can create a sense of rapport and connection. Pay attention to their body language, facial expressions, and vocal tone, and subtly adjust yours to match theirs. This can build trust and increase receptiveness to your message.

2. Use Visual Aids:

Visual aids can complement and enhance your nonverbal communication. Utilize images, videos, or slides to support your verbal message and capture attention. Visuals can evoke emotions and reinforce key points, making your message more persuasive.

3. Pay Attention to Microexpressions:

Microexpressions are fleeting facial expressions that can reveal true emotions. Training yourself to recognize and interpret microexpressions can help you gauge your audience's reactions and adjust your message accordingly. This awareness allows you to adapt your pre-suasive techniques in real-time.

4. Control your Gestures:

Use deliberate and purposeful gestures to emphasize key points and convey confidence. Avoid excessive or distracting movements that may detract from your message. A well-timed gesture can enhance the persuasive impact and direct attention to critical aspects of your pre-suasive message.

5. Practice Active Listening:

Active listening involves nonverbal cues such as nodding, leaning forward, and maintaining eye contact. Demonstrating engagement and attentiveness through nonverbal communication shows respect and encourages others to be receptive to your message. It also allows you to gather valuable information about your audience's preferences and concerns.

CONCLUSION

Mastering nonverbal communication in pre-suasion involves understanding the power of nonverbal cues and strategically using them to enhance persuasive impact. Facial expressions, body language, vocal tone, and personal appearance all contribute to the overall effectiveness of your messages. By aligning your nonverbal communication with your pre-suasive goals, you can establish trust, build rapport, and increase the likelihood of influencing others.

Chapter 18: Using Storytelling as a Pre-suasive Tool

Storytelling is a powerful tool that can capture attention, evoke emotions, and facilitate effective communication. When used strategically, storytelling can also be a pre-suasive technique that shapes perceptions and influences behavior. In this chapter, we will explore how storytelling can be utilized as a pre-suasive tool to enhance persuasion and achieve desired outcomes.

THE POWER OF STORYTELLING

Stories have been a part of human communication since the beginning of time. They have the ability to engage our imaginations, transport us to different worlds, and connect us on a deeper level. When it comes to persuasion, storytelling taps into our emotions, making it a highly effective tool. Stories are memorable because they activate multiple areas of the brain. They engage both the logical and emotional centers, creating a more holistic experience for the listener. By weaving relevant stories into our persuasive messages, we can increase their impact and make them more memorable.

KEY ELEMENTS OF A PRE-SUASIVE STORY

Crafting a pre-suasive story involves considering the following key elements:

1. Relevance

The story should be relevant to the persuasive message and the target audience. It should resonate with their values, needs, and desires. By making the story relatable, the listener is more likely to pay attention and connect with the message.

2. Characters

Characters in a story provide a relatable and human element to the persuasive message. The protagonist should represent the target audience, allowing listeners to empathize with their experiences and emotions. By creating well-developed characters, the story becomes more engaging and persuasive.

3. Conflict and Resolution

Every good story needs conflict to drive the plot forward. By presenting a problem or challenge, the listener becomes emotionally invested in finding a solution. The resolution should align with the persuasive message, demonstrating how the desired outcome can overcome the conflict.

4. Emotion

Emotion is a powerful tool in storytelling. By evoking emotions such as empathy, joy, or fear, the story becomes more impactful and memorable. Emotional connections influence decision-making processes and can shape perceptions in a pre-suasive manner.

5. Structure and Narrative

A well-structured narrative helps guide the listener through the story. By following a clear beginning, middle, and end, the story becomes easier to follow and comprehend. This structure also creates anticipation and suspense, keeping the listener engaged until the resolution.

STRATEGIC APPLICATIONS OF PRE-SUASIVE STORYTELLING

There are several ways to strategically apply storytelling as a pre-suasive tool:

1. Opening with a Compelling Story

At the beginning of a persuasive message, starting with a compelling story can capture attention and set the tone for the rest of the communication. This establishes an emotional connection and primes the listener for the desired message.

2. Using Stories to Illustrate Benefits and Outcomes

Storytelling can be used to vividly depict the benefits and outcomes of the desired action or belief. By painting a picture of the positive results that can be achieved, the listener is more likely to be persuaded to take the desired course of action.

3. Addressing Objections and Concerns through Stories

Using stories to address objections and concerns can help alleviate any doubts or hesitations the listener may have. By presenting a story that addresses similar concerns and demonstrates a positive outcome, the listener's objections can be preemptively addressed.

4. Building Brands and Emotional Connections

Storytelling is a powerful tool for building brands and creating emotional connections with the audience. By sharing stories that align with the brand's values and mission, a deeper connection can be fostered, leading to increased trust and loyalty.

SUMMARY

Storytelling is a pre-suasive tool that can enhance persuasion and influence. By utilizing the power of storytelling, we can captivate attention, evoke emotions, and shape perceptions. Understanding the key elements of a pre-suasive story and strategically applying storytelling techniques can make our persuasive messages more engaging, memorable, and effective in achieving desired outcomes.

Chapter 19: Pre-suasive Marketing Strategies

In today's highly competitive market, businesses need to employ effective marketing strategies to capture the attention of their target audience and persuade them to take action. Pre-suasive marketing strategies, which involve shaping the perception of consumers before presenting the actual message, can significantly enhance the effectiveness of marketing efforts. This chapter will delve into various pre-suasive marketing strategies that organizations can utilize to influence consumer behavior and achieve their marketing objectives.

THE POWER OF PRE-SUASION IN MARKETING

Pre-suasive marketing is all about creating the right mindset in consumers before introducing a message. It involves understanding the target audience and crafting persuasive messages that align with their values, motivations, and desires. By strategically priming consumers with specific ideas or emotions, marketers can subtly influence their decision-making process. One of the key principles in pre-suasive marketing is the concept of attention redirection. By redirecting consumers' attention towards specific aspects of a product or service, marketers can effectively highlight its unique features and benefits. This can be achieved through clever positioning, creative packaging, and compelling visuals that capture the attention and curiosity of consumers.

SEGMENTATION AND TARGETING

To effectively utilize pre-suasive marketing strategies, it is crucial for businesses to first identify and understand their target audience. This involves segmenting the market based on various demographic, psychographic, and behavioral factors. By tailoring marketing messages to specific segments, businesses can better align their communication with the needs and preferences of their audience. Segmentation also allows businesses to identify key influencers within their target segments. These influencers can play a vital role in pre-suasion, as their opinions and recommendations can sway the perceptions and behaviors of other consumers. Collaborating with influencers and leveraging their authority can significantly enhance the effectiveness of pre-suasive marketing campaigns.

BUILDING BRAND TRUST AND CREDIBILITY

Trust and credibility are essential elements in any marketing strategy. Consumers are more likely to engage with brands they trust and perceive as credible. In pre-suasive marketing, establishing trust and credibility can be achieved through various strategies. One approach is to incorporate testimonials and endorsements from satisfied customers or industry experts. Sharing positive experiences and recommendations from credible sources can instill confidence in consumers and enhance their perception of the brand. Another strategy is to provide evidence of the brand's expertise and authority in the industry. This can be done by showcasing relevant certifications, awards, or partnerships with reputable organizations. Demonstrating thought leadership through informative content and educational resources can also help build credibility.

ELICITING EMOTIONS AND CREATING EMOTIONAL CONNECTIONS

Emotions play a significant role in consumer decision-making. Pre-suasive marketing strategies can tap into these emotions and create emotional connections with consumers, which can positively influence their perception of a brand or product. One way to elicit emotions is through storytelling. By weaving relatable narratives that evoke specific emotions, marketers can engage consumers on a deeper level and make their messages more memorable. Emotional storytelling can create an emotional bond between the brand and the consumer, leading to increased brand loyalty and advocacy. In addition to storytelling, visual elements such as colors, images, and videos can also elicit emotions and enhance pre-suasive marketing efforts. Using visuals that evoke the desired emotional response can help create a positive association with the brand and influence consumer behavior.

UTILIZING SOCIAL PROOF AND SOCIAL INFLUENCE

Social proof is a powerful tool in pre-suasive marketing. People tend to look to others for guidance and validation, especially in uncertain situations. By showcasing positive social proof such as customer reviews, ratings, or social media mentions, marketers can leverage social influence to sway the perceptions and behaviors of potential customers. Incorporating user-generated content, such as customer testimonials or user reviews, can also enhance social proof and build trust. Consumers are more likely to trust the opinions and experiences of their peers, making user-generated content a valuable pre-suasive marketing strategy.

CREATING SCARCITY AND URGENCY

Scarcity and urgency are psychological triggers that can significantly impact consumer behavior. By creating a sense of scarcity or limited availability, marketers can tap into consumers' fear of missing out and motivate them to take action. Limited time offers, flash sales, or exclusive deals are examples of pre-suasive marketing strategies that leverage scarcity and urgency. By highlighting the limited availability of a product or service, marketers can generate a sense of urgency and drive consumers to make a purchase decision.

PERSONALIZATION AND TAILORING MESSAGES

Pre-suasive marketing is most effective when messages are personalized and tailored to individual consumers. By understanding the unique needs, preferences, and motivations of their target audience, marketers can create personalized messages that resonate on a deeper level. Personalization can involve addressing consumers by their name, referencing their previous interactions or purchases, and providing tailored recommendations based on their preferences. By showing consumers that the brand understands and cares about their individual needs, marketers can create a sense of trust and connection.

MEASURING AND OPTIMIZING PRE-SUASIVE MARKETING STRATEGIES

As with any marketing strategy, it is important to measure the effectiveness of pre-suasive marketing efforts and optimize them for maximum impact. Key performance indicators (KPIs) such as conversion rates, click-through rates, and engagement metrics can provide insights into the success of pre-suasive marketing campaigns. By analyzing data and feedback, marketers can identify areas for improvement and refine their pre-suasive marketing strategies. A/B testing can be used to compare different approaches and determine the most effective messaging, visuals, or offers.

Final Thoughts

Pre-suasive marketing strategies have the potential to significantly impact consumer behavior and improve marketing effectiveness. By understanding the power of pre-suasion and implementing tailored strategies, businesses can enhance their ability to influence consumer decision-making and achieve their marketing objectives. In the next chapter, we will explore how pre-suasion can be applied in sales and negotiation contexts. Stay tuned for valuable insights and strategies to improve your persuasive abilities.

Chapter 20: Pre-suasion in Sales and Negotiation

In the world of sales and negotiation, the ability to effectively persuade and influence others is crucial for achieving successful outcomes. Pre-suasion, the art of shaping someone's perception or mindset before introducing a persuasive message, plays a significant role in these contexts. By understanding and strategically applying pre-suasion techniques, salespeople and negotiators can increase their effectiveness and improve their chances of achieving desired outcomes.

THE POWER OF PRE-SUASION IN SALES

In sales, the key objective is to convince potential customers to make a purchase. Pre-suasion can significantly impact the outcome of a sales pitch by priming customers and directing their attention towards specific ideas or emotions. By creating the right pre-suasive mindset, salespeople can increase the likelihood of closing a sale. One important aspect of pre-suasion in sales is understanding the target audience. By conducting thorough research and analysis, salespeople can identify the motivations, needs, and pain points of potential customers. This information can then be used to tailor the sales message and align it with the customer's values and desires. Emotional appeal is another powerful tool in pre-suasive sales techniques. By appealing to the customer's emotions, salespeople can create a connection and build rapport. This can be achieved through storytelling, using vivid language, and highlighting the potential benefits and outcomes of the product or service being sold. Another pre-suasive strategy in sales is providing social proof. By showcasing testimonials, reviews, or case studies from satisfied customers, salespeople can leverage the power of social influence. When potential customers see that others have had a positive experience with a product or service, they are more likely to trust the salesperson and consider making a purchase. Addressing potential concerns or objections is also crucial in pre-suasive sales techniques. By anticipating and proactively addressing any hesitations or doubts, salespeople can alleviate customer fears and increase their confidence in the product or service.

PRE-SUASION TECHNIQUES IN NEGOTIATION

Negotiation involves reaching an agreement between parties where each party aims to maximize their own interests. In this context, pre-suasion can be used to influence the negotiation process and achieve desired outcomes. One pre-suasive technique in negotiation is the concept of priming. By priming the other party before the negotiation begins, negotiators can subtly direct their attention towards specific ideas or concepts that are advantageous to their own position. This can be done through initial conversations and interactions that subtly introduce relevant information or emphasize certain perspectives. Another pre-suasive strategy in negotiation is the use of cognitive biases. By understanding and leveraging common biases such as anchoring, confirmation bias, or loss aversion, negotiators can shape the other party's perception of value and influence their decision-making process. For example, by starting the negotiation with a high anchor value, negotiators can influence the other party to perceive subsequent offers as more favorable. Building trust and establishing a positive relationship is also important in pre-suasive negotiation techniques. By demonstrating credibility, understanding the other party's needs and concerns, and showing a willingness to cooperate, negotiators can create a favorable environment for reaching mutually beneficial agreements. Active listening and empathy are essential pre-suasive skills in negotiation. By genuinely understanding and acknowledging the other party's perspective, negotiators can build rapport and increase the likelihood of finding solutions that meet both parties' interests.

MEASURING AND IMPROVING PRE-SUASION IN SALES AND NEGOTIATION

Measuring the effectiveness of pre-suasion techniques in sales and negotiation is crucial for continuous improvement and optimization. Salespeople and negotiators can track key metrics such as conversion rates, sales volume, customer satisfaction, or negotiation outcomes to evaluate the impact of pre-suasion strategies. Feedback from customers or negotiation counterparts can also provide valuable insights into the effectiveness of pre-suasive techniques. By actively seeking feedback and adjusting the approach based on the responses received, salespeople and negotiators can refine their pre-suasion strategies and improve their overall performance. To further enhance the effectiveness of pre-suasion in sales and negotiation, ongoing learning and development are essential. By staying up-to-date with the latest research, attending training programs, and seeking guidance from experienced professionals, salespeople and negotiators can continue to refine their pre-suasion skills and stay ahead in their fields.

Conclusion

Pre-suasion plays a powerful role in sales and negotiation, enabling professionals to shape perceptions, influence decision-making processes, and increase the likelihood of achieving desired outcomes. By understanding and strategically applying pre-suasion techniques, salespeople and negotiators can enhance their effectiveness, build stronger relationships, and ultimately achieve greater success in their endeavors. Continuous learning, feedback, and adaptation are key to mastering the art of pre-suasive sales and negotiation.

Chapter 21: Pre-suasive Leadership

In this chapter, we will explore the concept of pre-suasive leadership and how it can be applied to effectively influence and guide others. Leadership involves inspiring and motivating individuals to achieve common goals, and pre-suasion can be a powerful tool for persuasive leaders.

THE ROLE OF PRE-SUASION IN LEADERSHIP

Leadership is not just about giving orders or making decisions; it is about inspiring and influencing others to follow a particular direction. Pre-suasion can play a significant role in leadership by shaping the mindset and perception of followers before introducing a persuasive message or directive. Pre-suasive leaders understand that influencing others starts before the actual communication takes place. They strategically set the stage by redirecting attention, evoking specific emotions, and priming the audience to be more receptive to their message. By creating a pre-suasive environment, leaders can ensure that their message has a greater impact and is more likely to be accepted.

BUILDING TRUST AND CREDIBILITY

Trust and credibility are essential elements of leadership. Pre-suasive leaders focus on building trust and establishing credibility with their followers. They understand that without trust, their influence and ability to persuade others will be limited. To build trust, pre-suasive leaders must be honest, transparent, and consistent in their actions. They should demonstrate competence and knowledge in their field and show empathy and understanding towards their followers. By consistently displaying these qualities, leaders can gain the trust and respect of their team, making them more likely to be influenced and persuaded.

UTILIZING EMOTIONAL INTELLIGENCE

Emotional intelligence is a key skill for pre-suasive leaders. They have a deep understanding of their own emotions and the emotions of others. By leveraging emotional intelligence, leaders can connect with their followers on an emotional level, making their persuasive messages more impactful. Pre-suasive leaders are able to empathize with their team members and understand their needs and motivations. They utilize emotional appeals to inspire and motivate their followers, tapping into their emotions to create a sense of purpose and drive. By aligning their message with the emotional needs of their team, leaders can successfully influence and persuade others.

CREATING A VISION AND DIRECTION

One of the core responsibilities of leaders is to create and communicate a compelling vision and direction for their team. Pre-suasive leaders understand the importance of crafting a persuasive message that aligns with the values and aspirations of their followers. They use pre-suasion techniques to capture attention, build interest, and establish credibility. By framing their message in a way that resonates with their team, leaders can inspire and motivate them to work towards a common goal. They leverage storytelling, emotional appeals, and social proof to create a vision that is compelling and persuasive.

NURTURING RELATIONSHIPS AND COLLABORATION

Pre-suasive leaders recognize the importance of building strong relationships with their team members. They understand that by cultivating positive connections, they can increase their influence and persuasive abilities. Leadership is not just about giving orders; it is about fostering collaboration and teamwork. Pre-suasive leaders create an environment where individuals feel valued and heard. They actively listen to their team members, seek their input, and involve them in the decision-making process. By establishing collaborative relationships, leaders can gain the trust and commitment of their followers, making them more likely to be persuaded and influenced.

CONCLUSION

Pre-suasive leadership involves utilizing pre-suasion techniques to effectively influence and guide others. By strategically shaping the mindset and perception of their followers, pre-suasive leaders can increase their persuasive abilities and achieve greater success in their leadership roles. Leadership is not just about authority; it is about understanding and connecting with others. By utilizing pre-suasion, leaders can create a positive and engaging environment that fosters collaboration and inspires action. Pre-suasive leadership is a powerful tool for individuals who want to become influential and effective leaders.

Chapter 22: Applying Pre-suasion in Personal Relationships

In this chapter, we will explore how pre-suasion can be applied in personal relationships to enhance communication, build trust, and strengthen connections with others. Pre-suasion is not only useful in professional settings but can also be a powerful tool in our personal lives.

THE POWER OF PRE-SUASION IN PERSONAL RELATIONSHIPS

Pre-suasion in personal relationships involves shaping someone's perception or mindset before introducing a persuasive message or attempting to influence their behavior. By strategically priming individuals, we can pave the way for more effective and successful communication. When engaging with our loved ones, it's important to understand their values, motivations, and emotional triggers. These insights allow us to tailor our approach to align with their desires and needs, making them more receptive to our messages. By employing pre-suasion techniques, we can foster a deeper understanding and connection with those closest to us.

BUILDING TRUST AND CONNECTION

Trust is the foundation of any healthy relationship, and pre-suasion can help establish and strengthen that trust. By consistently demonstrating honesty, reliability, and genuine care, we can create a sense of trustworthiness that makes our loved ones more inclined to listen and consider our perspectives. Effective pre-suasion in personal relationships involves active listening, empathy, and understanding. By truly hearing and acknowledging our loved ones' thoughts and feelings, we show them that their opinions matter and that we value their input. This can enhance the quality of our interactions and foster a deeper sense of connection.

CREATING POSITIVE EMOTIONAL ASSOCIATIONS

Emotions play a significant role in personal relationships, and pre-suasion can leverage these emotions to create positive associations. By intentionally evoking emotions such as love, joy, and gratitude, we can shape the emotional climate of our relationships. One effective technique is to use storytelling to elicit emotions and make our messages more impactful. Sharing personal anecdotes or relatable stories helps our loved ones connect with us on an emotional level, making it easier for them to understand our perspective and be influenced by it.

INFLUENCING BEHAVIOR IN A POSITIVE WAY

Pre-suasion in personal relationships should always be used ethically and with positive intentions. Instead of coercing or manipulating our loved ones, we should strive to guide their behavior towards positive outcomes and personal growth. By highlighting the benefits and rewards of a particular course of action, we can motivate our loved ones to make choices that align with their goals and values. It's essential to respect their autonomy and allow them to make their own decisions, rather than trying to control or force them.

HANDLING RESISTANCE AND CONFLICT

Even with effective pre-suasive techniques, disagreements and conflicts are bound to arise in personal relationships. It's crucial to approach these challenges with empathy, patience, and respect for the other person's perspective. When faced with resistance, active listening becomes even more important. By truly understanding the reasons behind someone's resistance, we can address their concerns and find common ground. Demonstrating flexibility and a willingness to compromise can help us find win-win solutions that strengthen the relationship.

NURTURING LONG-TERM RELATIONSHIPS

Pre-suasion in personal relationships is not just about short-term persuasion; it's about fostering lasting connections. It's important to take a long-term perspective and invest in ongoing communication and understanding. By consistently applying pre-suasive techniques, we can maintain the quality of our relationships, adapt to any changes or challenges, and continue to influence and support our loved ones in a positive way.

CONCLUSION

Applying pre-suasion in personal relationships can enhance communication, build trust, and strengthen connections. By understanding the values, motivations, and emotions of our loved ones, we can tailor our approach to be more effective in influencing their behavior and actions. However, it's essential to use pre-suasive techniques ethically and with the best interests of our loved ones in mind. By nurturing long-term relationships and investing in ongoing communication, we can create deeper and more fulfilling connections with those who matter most to us.

Chapter 23: Pre-suasion in Politics and Public Speaking

Public speaking and politics are two arenas where effective persuasion can make a significant impact. Pre-suasion techniques can be utilized in these contexts to shape perceptions, influence decision-making, and inspire action. Whether it's delivering a compelling speech or running a political campaign, understanding the principles of pre-suasion can greatly enhance success.

THE POWER OF PRE-SUASION IN POLITICS

In politics, pre-suasion plays a vital role in swaying public opinion and garnering support. By framing the narrative and shaping the context, politicians can prime voters to be more receptive to their messages. Here are some key aspects of pre-suasion in politics:

1. Framing the Narrative

Politicians often use framing techniques to present their ideas and policies in a favorable light. By highlighting certain aspects and downplaying others, they shape the way voters perceive the issue. For example, framing a tax policy as "fair and equitable" rather than "burdensome" can elicit a more positive response from the public.

2. Emotion as a Persuasive Tool

Emotions have a powerful impact on decision-making, and politicians understand this well. They use emotional appeals to connect with voters on a deeper level. Whether it's invoking hope, fear, or empathy, emotions can sway public opinion and inspire action.

3. Social Proof and Endorsements

Endorsements from influential individuals or trusted organizations can enhance a politician's credibility and persuade voters. People often look to others for guidance and validation in their decision-making process. By leveraging social proof, politicians can tap into the power of endorsement and increase their persuasive influence.

PRE-SUASION IN PUBLIC SPEAKING

Public speaking is a platform that allows individuals to influence and inspire others. Whether it's a TED talk, a business presentation, or a motivational speech, pre-suasion techniques can be employed to captivate the audience and deliver a memorable message. Here are some key strategies for pre-suasion in public speaking:

1. Captivating Attention from the Start

The opening moments of a speech are critical for capturing the audience's attention. Pre-suasive speakers use powerful statements, intriguing questions, or compelling anecdotes to engage their listeners right from the beginning. By piquing curiosity or evoking emotions, they lay the foundation for a persuasive delivery.

2. Building Rapport and Credibility

Establishing trust and credibility is essential for effective persuasion. Pre-suasive speakers focus on building rapport with their audience by connecting on a personal level, sharing relatable stories, or demonstrating expertise in their field. This helps create a strong foundation of trust and makes the audience more receptive to their message.

3. Crafting a Compelling Narrative

Storytelling is a powerful tool in pre-suasive public speaking. Narratives have the ability to evoke emotions, create empathy, and make the message more relatable. Pre-suasive speakers incorporate storytelling techniques to illustrate their points, provide real-life examples, and create a memorable experience for the audience.

4. Utilizing Visual Aids and Nonverbal Communication

Visual aids, such as slides or props, can enhance the impact of a speech. They can help convey complex information, provide visual stimulation, and reinforce key points. Additionally, nonverbal cues such as body language, facial expressions, and vocal tone play a crucial role in pre-suasive public speaking. They can convey confidence, authenticity, and passion, enhancing the speaker's persuasive influence.

5. Call to Action and Follow-Up

A pre-suasive speech should always include a clear call to action. Whether it's inspiring the audience to take a specific action, adopt a certain mindset, or support a cause, a well-crafted call to action can motivate the audience to act upon the message. Additionally, following up after the speech, providing additional resources or engagement opportunities, can further reinforce the persuasive impact.

CONCLUSION

Pre-suasion has a significant role to play in both politics and public speaking. By understanding and leveraging pre-suasion techniques, politicians can shape public opinion and influence decision-making processes. Similarly, in public speaking, pre-suasion can be used to captivate audiences, build credibility, and deliver impactful messages. The power of pre-suasion in these contexts highlights its effectiveness as a strategic tool for persuasion and influence.

Chapter 24: Pre-suasive Techniques for Influence and Persuasion

In this chapter, we will explore various pre-suasive techniques that can be used to enhance influence and persuasion. Pre-suasion is the act of shaping someone's perception or mindset before introducing a persuasive message. By strategically directing attention and priming individuals with specific ideas or emotions, we can increase the effectiveness of our persuasive efforts. Let's dive into some key pre-suasive techniques:

UTILIZING COGNITIVE BIASES

Cognitive biases are systematic patterns of deviation from rationality in judgment and decision-making. Understanding these biases can help us leverage them in pre-suasive communication. Here are a few cognitive biases commonly used in pre-suasion:

Confirmation Bias

Confirmation bias is the tendency to search for, interpret, favor, and recall information in a way that confirms one's preexisting beliefs. In pre-suasion, we can present information that aligns with the target audience's existing beliefs to reinforce their current perspectives.

Anchoring Bias

Anchoring bias is the tendency to rely heavily on the first piece of information encountered when making decisions. In pre-suasion, we can use an initial anchor to influence subsequent judgments and decisions. By introducing a high-value option or presenting the desired outcome as the default choice, we can influence the target audience's decision-making.

Availability Heuristic

The availability heuristic is the mental shortcut people use to estimate the likelihood or frequency of an event based on how easily examples or instances come to mind. In pre-suasion, we can prime individuals with relevant examples or stories that evoke specific emotions or associations to influence their decision-making.

Social Proof Bias

Social proof bias is the tendency to conform to the actions or beliefs of others. In pre-suasion, we can leverage social proof by highlighting the actions or beliefs of influential individuals or groups to encourage conformity. Testimonials, endorsements, or case studies can be powerful tools in leveraging social proof.

Recency Bias

Recency bias is the tendency to weigh the most recent information more heavily when making decisions. In pre-suasion, we can present the most compelling information right before the moment of decision to increase its impact and influence the target audience's choice.

Loss Aversion

Loss aversion is the tendency to prefer avoiding losses over acquiring equivalent gains. In pre-suasion, we can frame the persuasive message in terms of potential losses to trigger motivation and increase the target audience's receptiveness to our message.

Authority Bias

Authority bias is the tendency to attribute greater accuracy to the opinion or actions of an authority figure. In presuasion, we can incorporate endorsements or testimonials from credible individuals or institutions to enhance our credibility and increase the trust and compliance of the target audience. Understanding and applying these cognitive biases in a responsible and ethical manner can significantly enhance our influence and persuasion efforts.

CRAFTING POWERFUL AND PERSUASIVE MESSAGES

Crafting pre-suasive messages that resonate with the target audience is paramount in effective persuasion. Here are some strategies to consider:

Understand Your Target Audience

To craft a powerful pre-suasive message, it's crucial to have a deep understanding of your target audience. Consider their values, beliefs, motivations, and pain points. Tailor your message to align with their needs and desires.

Use Emotional Appeal

Emotions play a significant role in decision-making. Use emotional appeals to evoke specific emotions that align with your desired outcome. Highlight the emotional benefits or consequences of your message to make it more impactful.

Create a Compelling Narrative

Storytelling is a powerful tool in pre-suasion. Craft a compelling narrative that captivates your audience's attention and creates an emotional connection. Use vivid language and relatable characters to make your message more engaging and memorable.

Provide Social Proof

Social proof can be a persuasive technique in pre-suasion. Highlight testimonials, reviews, or endorsements from satisfied customers or influential individuals to build trust and credibility.

Highlight Benefits and Rewards

Focus on the benefits and rewards of your message. Clearly communicate how your proposition can improve their lives or solve their problems. Emphasize the positive outcomes they can expect to achieve.

Address Potential Concerns

Anticipate and address potential concerns or objections that your audience may have. By proactively addressing these concerns, you can alleviate doubts and increase the likelihood of acceptance.

Keep It Simple and Clear

Complex messages are harder to process and comprehend. Keep your message simple, concise, and easy to understand. Use clear language and avoid jargon or technical terms that may confuse your audience.

Test and Iterate Messaging Strategies

Effective pre-suasive messaging requires continuous refinement and optimization. Test different messaging strategies, gather feedback, and iterate based on the results. A/B testing and customer feedback can provide valuable insights for improving your messaging effectiveness. By implementing these pre-suasive techniques and crafting powerful messaging, you can significantly enhance your influence and persuasion skills. Remember to use these techniques responsibly and ethically, always keeping the best interests of your audience in mind. The next chapter will explore how to captivate attention and build interest in pre-suasive communication.

Chapter 25: Ethics and Responsibility in Pre-suasion

Ethics and responsibility play a crucial role in the practice of pre-suasion. While pre-suasion techniques can be powerful tools for influence and persuasion, it is essential to use them in an ethical and responsible manner. In this chapter, we will dive deeper into the importance of ethics and responsibility in pre-suasion and explore strategies for practicing pre-suasion with integrity.

THE ETHICAL DILEMMA

When it comes to pre-suasion, there is often an ethical dilemma. On one hand, pre-suasion can be seen as manipulative and deceptive, as it involves shaping someone's perception or mindset before introducing a persuasive message. On the other hand, pre-suasion can also be viewed as a strategic communication tool that allows us to better understand our target audience and craft messages that resonate with them.

Responsible Use of Pre-suasion

To navigate this ethical dilemma, it is important to approach pre-suasion with responsibility and integrity. Here are some strategies for practicing pre-suasion responsibly: 1. Transparency: Be transparent about your intentions and the methods you are using to shape someone's perception. Clearly communicate the purpose of your persuasive message. 2. Informed Consent: Seek informed consent when utilizing pre-suasion techniques. Inform individuals about the methods you will be using and the potential impact it may have on their decision-making processes. 3. Respect Autonomy: Respect the autonomy of individuals by giving them the freedom to make their own decisions. Avoid using pre-suasion techniques to unduly influence or manipulate their choices. 4. Do No Harm: Ensure that your pre-suasion techniques do not harm or deceive individuals in any way. Avoid using fear-based tactics or misinformation to sway their decisions. 5. Long-Term Relationships: Focus on building long-term relationships rather than short-term gains. Prioritize the well-being and satisfaction of your target audience by providing value and addressing their needs. 6. Cultural Sensitivity: Consider the cultural context in which you are practicing pre-suasion. Be mindful of cultural norms and values while crafting your persuasive messages.

Ethical Considerations in Decision-Making

In addition to practicing pre-suasion responsibly, it is important to consider the ethical implications of the decisions we make as influencers and communicators. Here are some ethical considerations to keep in mind: 1. Honesty: Be honest and truthful in your pre-suasive messages. Avoid using misleading or inaccurate information to achieve your persuasive objectives. 2. Respect Diversity: Recognize and respect diverse perspectives and values. Ensure that your pre-suasive messages are inclusive and don't discriminate against any group or individual. 3. Minimize Harm: Strive to minimize harm and negative consequences that may arise from your pre-suasion techniques. Consider the potential unintended effects of your persuasive messages. 4. Accountability: Be accountable for the impact of your pre-suasion techniques. Regularly evaluate and reflect on the ethical implications of your persuasive practices. 5. Continuous Learning: Stay updated on ethical standards and best practices in the field of pre-suasion. Engage in continuous learning and improvement to enhance your ethical decision-making skills.

CONCLUSION

Ethics and responsibility are integral to the practice of pre-suasion. By practicing pre-suasion with transparency, informed consent, respect for autonomy, and a focus on long-term relationships, we can ensure that our persuasive efforts are ethical and responsible. It is important to continuously reflect on our ethical decision-making and strive to minimize harm while maximizing the positive impact of pre-suasion techniques.

Chapter 26: Overcoming Resistance to Pre-suasion

Pre-suasion is a powerful tool for shaping perceptions and influencing decision-making processes. However, it is important to recognize that not everyone will be receptive to pre-suasive techniques. Resistance to pre-suasion can come from various factors, such as personal beliefs, prior experiences, or skepticism towards manipulation. Overcoming resistance requires understanding and addressing these concerns while still maintaining ethical practices.

THE POWER OF EMPATHY

One of the key strategies for overcoming resistance to pre-suasion is the power of empathy. By putting ourselves in the shoes of those we are trying to persuade, we can gain a better understanding of their perspective and concerns. Empathy allows us to approach pre-suasion with respect and consideration for the individual's autonomy and values.

EDUCATING AND INFORMING

Resistance often stems from a lack of understanding or misinformation about pre-suasion techniques. Educating and informing individuals about the principles and strategies behind pre-suasion can help alleviate concerns and dispel misconceptions. By providing knowledge and transparency, we can build trust and credibility, increasing the likelihood of a positive reception to pre-suasion.

BUILDING RAPPORT AND TRUST

Building rapport and trust is crucial when overcoming resistance to pre-suasion. People are more likely to be persuaded by someone they trust and feel connected to. Taking the time to establish rapport, actively listening to their concerns, and addressing them in a respectful manner can help break down barriers and create a more receptive environment for pre-suasive messages.

PROVIDING EVIDENCE AND SOCIAL PROOF

Resistance to pre-suasion can often be overcome by providing evidence and social proof. Demonstrating the effectiveness and positive outcomes of pre-suasion techniques can help alleviate skepticism and generate trust. Sharing success stories, testimonials, or data-driven evidence can show the practical benefits of pre-suasion, making it easier for individuals to embrace.

RESPECTING AUTONOMY AND CONSENT

Respecting autonomy and obtaining consent are essential in overcoming resistance to pre-suasion. It is important to give individuals the freedom to make their own choices and decisions, even if they ultimately decide not to be persuaded. By respecting their autonomy and seeking their consent, we create an atmosphere of trust and mutual respect, allowing for more meaningful and ethical persuasion.

ADAPTING AND LEARNING FROM FEEDBACK

Another important aspect of overcoming resistance to pre-suasion is the ability to adapt and learn from feedback. By actively seeking feedback from individuals and being open to constructive criticism, we can refine our pre-suasive techniques and approaches. Continuous improvement and a willingness to adapt ensure that our pre-suasion efforts are effective and ethical.

CONCLUSION

Overcoming resistance to pre-suasion requires empathy, education, trust-building, providing evidence, respecting autonomy, and adapting based on feedback. By addressing concerns and engaging in open and transparent communication, we can create a more receptive environment for pre-suasive messages. Ultimately, it is important to approach pre-suasion with integrity, always placing the well-being and autonomy of individuals at the forefront.

Chapter 27: Analyzing and Measuring Pre-suasive Success

Analyzing and measuring the success of pre-suasive strategies is essential for understanding their impact and making informed decisions for future campaigns. Without proper analysis and measurement, it is difficult to determine whether pre-suasion techniques are effectively influencing perceptions and guiding behavior.

WHY ANALYZING AND MEASURING PRE-SUASIVE SUCCESS IS IMPORTANT

Analyzing and measuring pre-suasive success provides valuable insights into the effectiveness of persuasion techniques. It allows us to identify what is working well and what needs improvement. By understanding the impact of pre-suasion, we can refine our strategies, increase our persuasive power, and achieve better results. When pre-suasive techniques are correctly utilized, they can lead to increased engagement, stronger brand loyalty, higher conversion rates, and more positive customer experiences. However, without careful analysis and measurement, it is challenging to quantify these benefits and attribute them directly to pre-suasion efforts.

METHODS FOR ANALYZING PRE-SUASIVE SUCCESS

There are various methods for analyzing and measuring pre-suasive success, depending on the specific goals and objectives of the campaign. Here are some common approaches:

Data Collection and Analysis:

Collecting relevant data about the target audience and their behavior is crucial for determining the impact of pre-suasive strategies. This can include information such as demographic data, online interactions, conversion rates, and customer feedback. Analyzing this data can provide insights into the effectiveness of pre-suasion techniques and identify areas for improvement.

A/B Testing:

A/B testing involves creating two different versions of a pre-suasive message or campaign and testing them against each other to determine which is more effective. By comparing the performance of these variations, it becomes possible to identify the elements that contribute to successful pre-suasion and optimize future strategies accordingly.

Surveys and Interviews:

Gathering feedback directly from the target audience through surveys and interviews can provide valuable qualitative data about the impact of pre-suasion. By asking specific questions about their perceptions, attitudes, and behaviors, it becomes possible to gain deeper insights into the effectiveness of pre-suasive techniques and identify areas for improvement.

KEY METRICS FOR MEASURING PRE-SUASIVE SUCCESS

There are several key metrics that can be used to measure pre-suasive success. These metrics are often specific to the objectives of the campaign but can include: - Conversion rates: Measuring the percentage of individuals who take the desired action, such as making a purchase or subscribing to a newsletter, can indicate the effectiveness of pre-suasive strategies. - Click-through rates: Measuring the number of individuals who click on a pre-suasive message or call to action can provide insights into the appeal and engagement generated by the message. - Customer satisfaction: Measuring customer satisfaction through surveys or feedback can indicate whether pre-suasion efforts are positively impacting the overall customer experience. - Brand perception: Monitoring changes in brand perception, such as brand awareness, image, and reputation, can reveal the impact of pre-suasive strategies on shaping audience perceptions. - Return on investment: Assessing the financial impact of pre-suasive strategies by comparing the costs of implementation to the generated revenue can determine the return on investment and overall success of the campaign.

CONTINUOUS IMPROVEMENT AND OPTIMIZATION

Analyzing and measuring pre-suasive success is not a one-time process. It is an ongoing effort that requires continuous monitoring, analysis, and optimization. By regularly evaluating the effectiveness of pre-suasion techniques and making necessary adjustments, we can continually improve our persuasive strategies and achieve even better results over time. It is important to keep in mind that pre-suasion is not a one-size-fits-all approach. Different audiences, industries, and contexts may require different strategies and metrics for analysis. By tailoring our approach to the specific goals and objectives of each campaign, we can maximize the impact of pre-suasion and achieve meaningful results. In conclusion, analyzing and measuring pre-suasive success is vital for understanding the impact and effectiveness of persuasion techniques. By collecting and analyzing data, conducting A/B tests, and gathering feedback, we can determine the success of pre-suasive campaigns. Key metrics such as conversion rates, click-through rates, customer satisfaction, brand perception, and return on investment provide insights into the effectiveness of pre-suasion techniques. Continuously evaluating and optimizing pre-suasion efforts allows for continuous improvement and enhanced persuasive power.

Chapter 28: Common Pitfalls and Mistakes in Pre-suasion

Pre-suasion is a powerful technique that can significantly influence others and increase the effectiveness of our persuasive efforts. However, like any strategy, there are common pitfalls and mistakes that one should be aware of to avoid undermining the potential impact of pre-suasion. In this chapter, we will explore some of these common pitfalls and provide insights on how to navigate them successfully.

1. LACK OF CLEAR OBJECTIVES

One of the most common mistakes in pre-suasion is not having clear objectives. Without a clear understanding of what you want to achieve, it becomes difficult to design an effective pre-suasive message. Before diving into pre-suasion, take the time to define your goals and desired outcomes. This will help you tailor your message and strategies accordingly.

2. FAILURE TO UNDERSTAND THE TARGET AUDIENCE

Another pitfall in pre-suasion is not understanding the target audience. Each individual or group has unique values, motivations, and preferences. By neglecting to understand their needs, you risk crafting messages that are ineffective or even alienating. Take the time to conduct research, gather insights, and empathize with your target audience. This will enable you to tailor your pre-suasive messages in a way that resonates with them.

3. OVERUSE OF COGNITIVE BIASES

Cognitive biases can be powerful tools in pre-suasion, but they should be utilized ethically and responsibly. It's important to remember that pre-suasion is about positive influence, not manipulation. Overusing cognitive biases can erode trust and credibility, ultimately undermining the effectiveness of your persuasive efforts. Strive for a balanced approach and use cognitive biases sparingly and transparently.

4. LACK OF AUTHENTICITY AND TRANSPARENCY

Authenticity and transparency are key factors in building trust and credibility. If your pre-suasive messages come across as deceitful or manipulative, they will likely be met with resistance. Be honest, transparent, and genuine in your communication. This will not only foster trust but also enhance the likelihood of achieving your desired persuasive outcomes.

5. INEFFECTIVE USE OF EMOTIONAL APPEALS

Emotional appeals are powerful in pre-suasion, but they need to be used effectively. It's important to strike the right balance between evoking emotions and maintaining rationality. Overly emotional appeals can cloud judgment and lead to impulsive decisions that are later regretted. Always ensure that your emotional appeals are grounded in logic and reason, providing a compelling and balanced argument.

6. LACK OF CONSISTENCY AND COHESION

Consistency and cohesion are crucial in pre-suasion. Your pre-suasive messages should align with your overall brand, values, and objectives. Inconsistencies can confuse and undermine the effectiveness of your persuasion efforts. Ensure that your pre-suasive messages are consistent across different channels and touchpoints, reinforcing the desired perceptions and actions.

7. FAILURE TO ADAPT AND LEARN FROM FEEDBACK

Continuous improvement is essential in pre-suasion. Failing to adapt and learn from feedback can lead to stagnant and ineffective persuasive efforts. Pay close attention to the responses and reactions of your target audience. Gather feedback, analyze data, and be willing to adjust your pre-suasion strategies accordingly. This flexibility and adaptability will help enhance the effectiveness of your persuasion techniques.

CONCLUSION

Avoiding these common pitfalls and mistakes in pre-suasion can significantly increase your chances of achieving your persuasive goals. By setting clear objectives, understanding your target audience, using cognitive biases ethically, being authentic and transparent, effectively using emotional appeals, maintaining consistency, and embracing continuous improvement, you can maximize the impact and effectiveness of your pre-suasion strategies. In the next chapter, we will explore psychological tricks and mind hacks for pre-suasion.

Chapter 29: Psychological Tricks and Mind Hacks for Pre-suasion

In the world of persuasion, understanding how the human mind works can be a powerful tool. By diving into the realm of psychology, we can uncover various tricks and mind hacks that can enhance our pre-suasion techniques. These psychological principles can help us shape perceptions, redirect attention, and influence decision-making processes. In this chapter, we will explore some of these tricks and hacks and learn how to apply them effectively in pre-suasive communication.

1. ANCHORING BIAS

One powerful psychological trick is the anchoring bias. This bias occurs when individuals rely too heavily on the first piece of information they receive when making decisions or judgments. By strategically presenting an anchor, you can influence subsequent judgments in your favor. When applying the anchoring bias in pre-suasion, consider starting with a strong, positive point that aligns with your persuasive message. This creates a mental anchor for the audience and sets the stage for their perception of subsequent information. By framing the conversation around this initial anchor, you can guide their decision-making process in the desired direction.

2. SCARCITY PRINCIPLE

The scarcity principle is another powerful psychological trick that taps into people's fear of missing out. When something is perceived as rare or limited in quantity, it becomes more desirable. By creating a sense of urgency and scarcity around your persuasive message, you can increase its perceived value and compel people to take action. To leverage the scarcity principle in pre-suasion, highlight the limited availability of your product, service, or opportunity. Emphasize that it is exclusive, in high demand, or about to run out. This creates a psychological trigger that motivates individuals to act quickly before they miss out. However, it is important to use this trick ethically and honestly, ensuring that the scarcity is genuine and not artificially created.

3. PRIMING

Priming involves exposing individuals to stimuli that activate specific associations or emotions. By pre-activating certain concepts or feelings, you can influence how information is processed and interpreted. Priming can be a powerful pre-suasion technique to shape perceptions and guide decision-making processes. To effectively prime individuals, carefully choose the stimuli relevant to your persuasive message. This could include visual cues, verbal cues, or even specific situations. For example, if you want to prime someone to be more open-minded, you could expose them to images or statements that promote open-mindedness beforehand. By strategically priming their mindset, you increase the likelihood of successfully persuading them.

4. FRAMING

Framing involves presenting information in a way that influences perception and decision-making. The way something is framed can shape how individuals interpret and respond to it. By framing your message in a positive or negative light, you can guide people's emotions and thoughts in the desired direction. When using framing in pre-suasion, consider the desired outcome and how you want your audience to perceive the information. Highlight the positive aspects, benefits, and rewards if you want to create a positive frame. Conversely, if you want to highlight potential problems or consequences, emphasize the negative aspects. By framing your message strategically, you can influence how individuals perceive and respond to it.

5. SOCIAL PROOF

Social proof is a psychological principle that states individuals are more likely to conform to the actions or beliefs of others, especially when they are uncertain or in unfamiliar situations. By providing evidence that others have already taken a certain action or hold a specific belief, you can increase the likelihood of persuasion. To leverage social proof in pre-suasion, provide testimonials, endorsements, or case studies that highlight others' positive experiences or opinions. This demonstrates that your persuasive message has been well-received by others, increasing its credibility and appeal. When individuals see that people like them have already taken action or hold the same belief, they are more likely to follow suit.

CONCLUSION

Psychological tricks and mind hacks can significantly enhance the effectiveness of your pre-suasion techniques. By understanding the biases and triggers that influence human behavior, you can strategically design your persuasive messages to align with these principles. Anchoring bias, scarcity principle, priming, framing, and social proof are just a few examples of the psychological tricks you can implement in pre-suasive communication. However, it is crucial to use these techniques responsibly, ethically, and with the intention of positively influencing others.

Chapter 30: Pre-suasive Strategies for Online Marketing

In today's digital era, online marketing has become an essential tool for businesses to reach their target audience. With the vast amount of information available online, capturing the attention and influencing the decision-making process of consumers can be challenging. However, by applying pre-suasion strategies, marketers can effectively shape consumers' perceptions and increase the effectiveness of their online marketing efforts.

THE POWER OF ATTENTION REDIRECTION

One of the key principles of pre-suasion in online marketing is attention redirection. In a digital landscape saturated with information, capturing and maintaining consumers' attention is crucial. By redirecting their attention towards specific ideas or emotions, marketers can increase the likelihood of influencing their decision-making process. There are several strategies for redirecting attention in online marketing. One strategy is to use visual elements such as eye-catching imagery or videos that immediately grab the viewer's attention. This can be achieved through bold colors, animated graphics, or creative designs. Another strategy is to craft compelling headlines or subject lines that pique curiosity and entice the reader to click and learn more. Creating a sense of novelty or exclusivity can also capture attention, such as offering limited-time promotions or exclusive access to certain content or products.

THE ROLE OF PERSONALIZATION

Personalization is another important pre-suasive strategy in online marketing. By tailoring messages and experiences to individual consumers, marketers can create a sense of relevance and connection, which can increase engagement and influence decision-making. To effectively implement personalization in online marketing, businesses can leverage data and analytics to understand their target audience. By collecting and analyzing consumer data, marketers can gain insights into their preferences, behaviors, and needs. This information can then be used to personalize content, recommendations, and offers. For example, an e-commerce website can suggest products based on the customer's previous purchases or browsing history. Email marketing campaigns can be personalized by addressing recipients by name and offering personalized recommendations or discounts based on their interests and behaviors.

THE IMPACT OF SOCIAL PROOF

Social proof is a powerful psychological phenomenon that can significantly influence consumer behavior. In online marketing, leveraging social proof can enhance pre-suasion by demonstrating that others have had positive experiences or opinions about a product or service. There are several ways to incorporate social proof into online marketing strategies. Testimonials and reviews from satisfied customers can be prominently displayed on websites or product pages. Influencer marketing can be utilized, where influential individuals endorse or promote a product or service to their followers. Case studies and success stories can be shared to showcase real-life examples of the benefits or results achieved. Displaying customer ratings or social media shares can also provide evidence of positive experiences and create a sense of popularity and trust.

THE INFLUENCE OF FRAMING

Framing is another pre-suasive strategy that can be used in online marketing to shape consumers' perceptions and guide their decision-making. By presenting information in a certain way, marketers can influence how a message is interpreted and create a desired perception. There are different types of framing that can be used in online marketing. One common technique is to frame the message in terms of benefits and rewards. By highlighting the positive outcomes that consumers can expect from a product or service, marketers can create a positive association and motivate them to take action. Another approach is to frame the message in terms of potential problems or consequences. By emphasizing the negative impact of not using a product or service, marketers can create a sense of urgency and prompt consumers to take immediate action.

OPTIMIZING USER EXPERIENCE

Another important aspect of pre-suasive strategies for online marketing is optimizing the user experience. A website or online platform that provides a seamless and enjoyable experience can significantly impact consumers' perceptions and willingness to engage with the marketing message. To optimize the user experience, businesses can focus on several factors. Website design should be user-friendly, with intuitive navigation and clear calls-to-action that guide visitors towards desired actions. Loading times should be minimized to prevent frustration and encourage continued engagement. Mobile responsiveness is crucial, as a growing number of consumers access the internet through mobile devices. Personalization, as mentioned earlier, can also enhance the user experience by tailoring content and recommendations to individual preferences.

MEASURING AND ANALYZING PRE-SUASIVE STRATEGIES

Measuring the effectiveness of pre-suasive strategies in online marketing is essential for optimizing and improving future campaigns. There are various methods and metrics that marketers can utilize to analyze the impact of their pre-suasive efforts. Data analytics can provide valuable insights into consumer behavior, such as click-through rates, conversion rates, or time spent on a website. A/B testing can be conducted to compare the performance of different pre-suasive approaches and identify which strategies are the most effective. Feedback from customers, through surveys or reviews, can also provide valuable information on their perceptions and experiences. By continuously measuring and analyzing the effectiveness of pre-suasive strategies, marketers can make data-driven decisions and refine their online marketing efforts to achieve better results.

Conclusion

Pre-suasion strategies play a crucial role in online marketing by shaping consumers' perceptions and influencing their decision-making process. Attention redirection, personalization, social proof, framing, and optimizing user experience are key techniques that marketers can employ to enhance the effectiveness of their online marketing campaigns. By understanding the principles and strategies of pre-suasion, businesses can create persuasive online marketing messages that capture attention, build trust, and ultimately drive conversions and customer loyalty.

Chapter 31: Pre-suasion in Customer Experience

When it comes to building strong customer relationships and driving repeat business, pre-suasion plays a vital role in shaping the customer experience. By strategically influencing customers' perceptions and mindsets before they interact with a brand or make a purchase, businesses can create a positive and impactful customer journey. In this chapter, we will explore how pre-suasion can be applied to enhance the customer experience, improve customer satisfaction, and drive customer loyalty.

UNDERSTANDING THE CUSTOMER JOURNEY

To effectively apply pre-suasion in the customer experience, it is essential to understand the customer journey. The customer journey refers to the series of touchpoints and interactions a customer has with a brand from initial awareness to post-purchase engagement. By identifying the key touchpoints and understanding customers' motivations and needs at each stage, businesses can strategically apply pre-suasive techniques to influence customers' perceptions and actions.

DESIGNING PRE-SUASIVE TOUCHPOINTS

One of the key ways to apply pre-suasion in customer experience is through the design of pre-suasive touchpoints. Pre-suasive touchpoints are the specific interactions or moments where businesses can shape customers' perceptions and influence their decision-making process. These touchpoints can include website design, product packaging, customer onboarding experiences, and post-purchase follow-ups. When designing pre-suasive touchpoints, it is important to consider the following strategies:

1. Attention redirection:

Redirecting customers' attention towards key messages, benefits, or features that align with their needs and desires can help shape their perceptions and increase engagement. This can be done through visually appealing designs, compelling headlines, and clear calls-to-action that highlight the value proposition.

2. Personalization:

Tailoring the customer experience based on individual preferences and previous interactions can create a sense of personal connection and enhance customer satisfaction. Personalized recommendations, targeted emails, and customized product suggestions can make customers feel understood and valued.

3. Social proof:

Incorporating social proof in pre-suasive touchpoints can influence customers' perceptions and behaviors. Testimonials, reviews, case studies, and user-generated content can build trust, credibility, and a sense of community among customers.

4. Emotional appeal:

Using emotional appeals in pre-suasive touchpoints can create a memorable and impactful experience. Triggering positive emotions such as happiness, joy, or surprise can enhance customers' perceptions of the brand and increase their likelihood of positive engagement.

5. Consistency:

Ensuring consistency throughout the customer journey helps build trust and reinforce the brand's value proposition. Consistent messaging, design elements, and tone of voice across different touchpoints create a cohesive and reliable brand experience.

MEASURING PRE-SUASIVE IMPACT IN CUSTOMER EXPERIENCE

Measuring the impact of pre-suasion in customer experience is essential to understand the effectiveness of pre-suasive strategies and make data-driven decisions.

There are several key metrics that can be used to measure the pre-suasive impact, including: - Customer satisfaction: Assessing customer satisfaction levels through surveys, feedback, and reviews can provide insights into the effectiveness of pre-suasive touchpoints. - Customer retention: Tracking customer retention rates and analyzing repeat purchase behavior can indicate the strength of the pre-suasive strategies in driving customer loyalty. - Conversion rates: Monitoring conversion rates at different stages of the customer journey can highlight the impact of pre-suasion on customer decision-making. - Net Promoter Score (NPS): Using NPS surveys to measure customer loyalty and likelihood of recommending the brand can gauge the overall effectiveness of the pre-suasive customer experience. - Engagement metrics: Analyzing customer engagement metrics such as click-through rates, time spent on the website, and social media interactions can indicate the level of pre-suasive impact. By regularly measuring these metrics and analyzing the results, businesses can identify areas for improvement, optimize pre-suasive strategies, and enhance the overall customer experience.

CONCLUSION

Pre-suasion can significantly enhance the customer experience by strategically influencing customers' perceptions and behaviors at various touchpoints. By understanding the customer journey, designing pre-suasive touchpoints, and measuring the impact, businesses can create a personalized, engaging, and impactful customer experience that drives satisfaction, loyalty, and advocacy. Incorporating pre-suasion into the customer experience can help businesses stand out in a competitive market and foster long-term customer relationships.

Chapter 32: Pre-suasion in Digital Advertising

Digital advertising has become an integral part of modern marketing strategies. With the rise of technology and internet usage, businesses have shifted their focus to digital platforms to reach and engage with their target audience. Pre-suasion techniques can be effectively applied in digital advertising to capture attention, influence perceptions, and guide consumer behavior. In this chapter, we will explore the various strategies and tactics that can be employed to harness the power of pre-suasion in digital advertising.

THE POWER OF ATTENTION REDIRECTION

In the digital realm, attention is a scarce resource. With countless ads vying for attention online, it is crucial for advertisers to strategically redirect the audience's attention towards their message. Pre-suasion offers valuable insights into how attention can be effectively captured and maintained. By leveraging novelty, emotions, and relevant stimuli, advertisers can create a compelling initial impact that entices viewers to engage further. One effective strategy for capturing attention is through the use of visually striking elements. Creative and visually appealing designs can instantly draw the audience's eyes and encourage them to explore further. Incorporating interactive elements, such as quizzes or games, can also be an effective way to make ads more engaging and capture attention.

PERSONALIZATION AND RELEVANCE

Personalization is a powerful pre-suasion technique that can significantly enhance the effectiveness of digital advertising. By tailoring messages to the individual preferences, interests, and behaviors of the target audience, advertisers can create a sense of relevance and increase the likelihood of engagement and conversion. Data-driven personalization allows advertisers to deliver targeted content based on user demographics, browsing history, and previous interactions. By analyzing user data, advertisers can segment their audience into specific groups and deliver personalized ads that resonate with their unique needs and preferences. This level of personalization creates a sense of connection and increases the chances of a positive response.

THE INFLUENCE OF SOCIAL PROOF

Social proof is a psychological phenomenon that states people are more likely to adopt the beliefs or actions of others in uncertain situations. In the context of digital advertising, social proof can be a powerful pre-suasion technique to influence consumer behavior. Including testimonials, reviews, ratings, or endorsements from satisfied customers or industry experts can create social proof and build trust. When potential customers see others endorsing a product or service, it increases their confidence and likelihood of making a purchase. Incorporating social proof in digital advertising can significantly impact credibility, conversion rates, and brand perception.

CREATING EMOTIONAL CONNECTIONS

Emotions play a crucial role in decision-making, and digital advertisers can leverage this by creating emotional connections with their target audience. By strategically incorporating emotional appeals in their ads, advertisers can evoke specific emotions that align with their brand and desired outcomes. Using storytelling techniques can be particularly effective in creating emotional connections. By telling a compelling story that resonates with the audience's values, aspirations, or struggles, advertisers can capture their attention and engage their emotions. Emotional storytelling can foster empathy, create a bond with the brand, and increase the likelihood of desired actions.

OPTIMIZING USER EXPERIENCE

The user experience (UX) plays a vital role in the success of digital advertising campaigns. A seamless and user-friendly experience enhances engagement and maximizes the impact of pre-suasion techniques. Advertisers need to ensure their ads are optimized for different devices, load quickly, and provide a smooth interaction. Testing and measuring the user experience through A/B testing, heatmaps, or user feedback can provide valuable insights for optimization. Continuous improvement based on user data and feedback helps to refine the pre-suasive strategies, enhance user engagement, and drive desired actions.

MEASURING AND ANALYZING PRE-SUASIVE IMPACT

Measuring the impact of pre-suasion in digital advertising is essential to evaluate the effectiveness of strategies and optimize campaigns. Key metrics for measuring pre-suasive impact may include click-through rates, conversion rates, engagement rates, bounce rates, and return on investment. By analyzing these metrics, advertisers can identify which pre-suasion techniques are the most effective and make data-driven decisions on refining and optimizing their campaigns. Regular monitoring and analysis enable advertisers to adapt their strategies in response to changing market dynamics and consumer preferences.

CONCLUSION

Digital advertising offers immense opportunities for applying pre-suasion techniques to influence consumer behavior. By strategically redirecting attention, personalizing messages, leveraging social proof, creating emotional connections, optimizing the user experience, and measuring impact, advertisers can enhance the effectiveness of their digital advertising efforts. Harnessing the power of pre-suasion in digital advertising enables businesses to stand out in a competitive landscape and drive desired actions from their target audience. Stay tuned for the next chapter, where we will explore the concept of nudging behavior through pre-suasion.

Chapter 33: Nudging Behavior through Pre-suasion

Behavioral economics has shown us that human beings are not always rational decision makers. Our choices and actions can be influenced by various factors, often without us even realizing it. In this chapter, we will explore how pre-suasion can be used to nudge behavior in a desired direction. Nudging refers to the use of subtle cues or interventions to steer individuals towards making certain choices or taking specific actions. It is based on the idea that small changes in the context or presentation of information can have a significant impact on decision making. Pre-suasion provides a powerful framework for designing nudges that are both effective and ethically responsible. One key aspect of nudging behavior through pre-suasion is understanding the power of defaults. Defaults refer to the pre-selected options or settings that individuals are presented with when making a decision. Research has shown that people often stick with the default option simply because it requires less effort or cognitive load. By strategically setting defaults, we can influence behavior without restricting individuals' freedom of choice. For example, in organ donation programs, countries that have an opt-out system, where individuals are automatically considered donors unless they specifically opt out, have significantly higher rates of organ donation compared to countries with an opt-in system. This simple change in default option has led to a substantial increase in donor registration. Similar principles can be applied in various contexts, such as retirement savings plans or energy conservation programs. Another pre-suasive technique for nudging behavior is using social norms. Humans are social beings, and we tend to conform to the behavior or beliefs of others. By highlighting what is commonly done or accepted within a specific group, we can encourage individuals to align their behavior with the perceived norm. For instance, in hotel rooms, a pre-suasive message informing guests about the majority of people who choose to reuse their towels can significantly increase towel reuse rates. By emphasizing that the majority of guests participate in this behavior, individuals are more likely to feel the social pressure to do the same. In addition to defaults and social norms, leveraging the power of commitments and consistency can also be effective in nudging behavior. When individuals make a public or written commitment to a particular course of action, they are more likely to follow through with it due to the desire for consistency. Take, for example, online retailers who use pre-suasion techniques to increase cart conversion rates. By reminding customers of their previous commitment to purchase an item by adding it to their cart, they increase the likelihood of completing the purchase. This small reminder taps into the principle of consistency and nudges customers towards fulfilling their commitment. It is important to note that while nudging can be a powerful tool for behavior change, ethical considerations must guide its implementation. Nudging should never be manipulative or coercive. Instead, it should empower individuals to make choices that align with their values and best interests. In conclusion, nudging behavior through pre-suasion allows us to guide individuals towards desired actions or choices without removing their freedom of choice. By strategically leveraging defaults, social norms, and consistency, we can nudge behavior in a positive direction. However, it is crucial to always prioritize ethics and responsibility when applying these techniques.

Chapter 34: Pre-suasive Design in Product Development

Product development is a crucial stage in bringing a new product or service to the market. It involves designing, creating, and refining the features, functionalities, and overall user experience of the product. Pre-suasive design, in this context, refers to shaping the perception and mindset of potential users before they even interact with the product. By strategically incorporating pre-suasive techniques into the design process, product developers can optimize the effectiveness of their offerings and increase user satisfaction.

UNDERSTANDING PRE-SUASIVE DESIGN

Pre-suasive design goes beyond creating aesthetically pleasing products. It involves intentionally designing various aspects of the product to influence the user's emotions, thoughts, and behaviors. By leveraging cognitive biases, emotional appeals, and social influence, pre-suasive design aims to shape the user's perception and guide their decision-making process. When implementing pre-suasive design in product development, it is essential to consider the target audience and their specific needs, desires, and preferences. By understanding their motivations and values, product developers can tailor the design elements to align with those factors. This customization enhances the user's connection with the product and increases the likelihood of them adopting or purchasing it.

INCORPORATING COGNITIVE BIASES

Cognitive biases play a significant role in decision-making processes. By understanding these biases, product developers can design products that align with users' natural tendencies and increase the likelihood of positive outcomes. One cognitive bias that can be leveraged in pre-suasive design is the anchoring bias. This bias occurs when individuals rely heavily on the first piece of information they encounter when making decisions. Product developers can strategically present the most appealing or persuasive feature of their product early on to create a positive anchor in the user's mind. Another cognitive bias that can be utilized is the availability heuristic. This bias refers to the tendency to base judgments and decisions on easily accessible information. Pre-suasive design can involve providing examples, stories, or testimonials that highlight the benefits and positive experiences associated with the product. This primes the user to think of these positive instances, making them more likely to perceive the product favorably.

CREATING EMOTIONAL CONNECTIONS

Emotional connections play a crucial role in user engagement and product adoption. Product developers can utilize pre-suasive design to evoke specific emotions that align with the desired user experience. For example, if the goal is to create a sense of excitement and anticipation, the design elements can be tailored to elicit those emotions through color choices, visual stimuli, and interactive features. Storytelling is another powerful pre-suasive technique that can be incorporated into product design. By creating a narrative around the product, developers can evoke emotions and establish a deeper connection with the user. The story can highlight the problem the product solves, the journey of its creation, or the positive impact it has had on previous users. This storytelling approach makes the product more relatable and memorable.

DESIGNING FOR SOCIAL INFLUENCE

Social influence can significantly impact people's decision-making processes. Pre-suasive design can tap into this influence by incorporating elements that highlight social proof and endorsements. For example, displaying customer reviews, ratings, or testimonials can create a sense of trust and credibility in the product. Additionally, designing for social norms can shape user behavior. By highlighting the widespread use or acceptance of the product, developers can convey that it is the expected or desirable choice. This can be achieved through visual cues, such as showing the product being used by a diverse group of people or referencing its popularity among a specific community.

MEASURING PRE-SUASIVE DESIGN EFFECTIVENESS

Measuring the effectiveness of pre-suasive design in product development is crucial for optimizing its impact. Product developers can gather user feedback through surveys, interviews, or user testing to understand how the design elements are influencing perception and behavior. Analyzing metrics such as user engagement, conversion rates, and customer satisfaction can provide valuable insights into the success of the pre-suasive design techniques implemented. Regular iteration and refinement based on user feedback and data analysis are essential for improving pre-suasive design strategies. By continuously evaluating the effectiveness of the design elements and making adjustments as needed, product developers can ensure that the product is as pre-suasively impactful as possible.

CONCLUSION

Pre-suasive design in product development involves strategically shaping the user's perception and decision-making processes through the design elements of a product. By incorporating cognitive biases, creating emotional connections, and leveraging social influence, product developers can optimize the effectiveness of their offerings. Measuring the impact and iterating based on user feedback are vital for continual improvement. Pre-suasive design has the potential to enhance user satisfaction, increase adoption rates, and ultimately drive the success of the product.

Chapter 35: The Future of Pre-suasion: Trends and Innovations

The field of pre-suasion is constantly evolving and adapting to the changing landscape of communication and influence. As technology advances and our understanding of human psychology deepens, new trends and innovations are emerging that have the potential to revolutionize the way we approach persuasion. In this chapter, we will explore some of these exciting developments and discuss their implications for the future of pre-suasion.

THE RISE OF ARTIFICIAL INTELLIGENCE

One significant trend in pre-suasion is the integration of artificial intelligence (AI) into persuasive communication strategies. AI-powered algorithms can analyze vast amounts of data to identify patterns, predict behaviors, and develop personalized pre-suasive messages. By leveraging machine learning and natural language processing techniques, AI can tailor messages to individual preferences, increasing their relevance and effectiveness. For example, imagine receiving an email from an online retailer that not only recommends products based on your past purchases but also incorporates persuasive language that appeals to your specific motivations and desires. AI-powered chatbots can also engage in pre-suasive conversations with customers, providing personalized recommendations and suggestions. However, as AI becomes more prevalent in pre-suasion, ethical considerations must be taken into account. Ensuring transparency and obtaining informed consent are crucial to maintain trust with consumers. Balancing personalized messaging with privacy concerns will be a key challenge for businesses implementing AI in their pre-suasive strategies.

VIRTUAL AND AUGMENTED REALITY

Virtual and augmented reality (VR/AR) technologies are transforming the way we experience and interact with the world. These immersive technologies have the potential to revolutionize pre-suasive communication by creating highly engaging and persuasive environments. Imagine being able to step into a virtual showroom where you can try on clothes, test drive cars, or even tour a dream vacation destination. By immersing users in realistic simulations, VR/AR can evoke emotions, create a sense of presence, and guide decision-making in powerful ways. Additionally, VR/AR can be used to simulate scenarios and provide virtual training for pre-suasive communicators. This allows them to practice and refine their skills in a safe and controlled environment, improving their ability to influence others effectively.

NEUROMARKETING AND BRAIN-COMPUTER INTERFACES

Neuromarketing, a field that combines neuroscience and marketing, is unlocking new insights into human behavior and decision-making. By using technologies such as electroencephalography (EEG) and functional magnetic resonance imaging (fMRI), researchers can measure brain activity and identify neural correlates of pre-suasion.

These advancements in neuromarketing can help pre-suasive communicators understand how specific stimuli and messages impact the brain, allowing them to design more effective pre-suasive strategies. For example, measuring brain responses to different colors, images, or narratives can help identify the most engaging and impactful elements to include in pre-suasive messages. Innovations in brain-computer interfaces (BCIs) also hold promise for the future of pre-suasion. BCIs enable direct communication between the brain and external devices, opening up possibilities for personalized and seamless pre-suasive experiences. For instance, a device could detect the user's emotions and deliver pre-suasive messages tailored to their current state of mind.

ETHICAL CONSIDERATIONS AND RESPONSIBLE IMPLEMENTATION

As pre-suasion continues to evolve, it is essential to maintain a strong focus on ethics and responsible implementation. Pre-suasion should always be used in a way that respects individuals' autonomy, privacy, and well-being. Additionally, transparency and informed consent should be prioritized to build and maintain trust with consumers. Furthermore, pre-suasive communicators must also consider the potential negative consequences of their persuasive efforts. Avoiding manipulative tactics and ensuring that the pre-suasive techniques used align with ethical guidelines is crucial. The future of pre-suasion holds great promise, with advancements in AI, VR/AR, neuromarketing, and BCIs offering exciting opportunities for more effective and personalized persuasion. However, it is important to approach these trends and innovations with a responsible and ethical mindset to ensure positive outcomes for both individuals and businesses. In the next chapter, we will dive into real-life case studies and success stories that showcase the power of pre-suasion in various industries and contexts. Stay tuned to discover how pre-suasion has transformed the way organizations communicate and influence others.

Chapter 36: Pre-suasion Case Studies and Success Stories

In this chapter, we will explore real-world examples and success stories that highlight the power and effectiveness of pre-suasion. By examining case studies, we can gain valuable insights into how pre-suasion techniques have been applied in various industries and contexts to influence behavior and achieve persuasive objectives. These examples will demonstrate the practical application and impact of pre-suasion, inspiring readers to apply these strategies in their own lives.

CASE STUDY 1: APPLE'S PRODUCT LAUNCH EVENTS

Apple has mastered the art of pre-suasion through its highly anticipated product launch events. Months before the event, Apple builds anticipation and engages its audience by subtly hinting at new product releases through teaser campaigns and mysterious invitations. By creating a sense of exclusivity and excitement, Apple primes its audience to be receptive to their message. During the event itself, Apple strategically directs attention towards the features, design, and benefits of their products. They use captivating visuals, immersive demonstrations, and storytelling techniques to engage the audience emotionally. By evoking emotions like curiosity, desire, and awe, Apple creates a positive and receptive mindset, making their audience more likely to embrace their new products and create a buzz around them.

CASE STUDY 2: CHARITY: WATER'S STORYTELLING CAMPAIGN

Charity: Water is a nonprofit organization that provides clean and safe drinking water to people in developing countries. They have successfully utilized pre-suasion techniques in their storytelling campaigns to engage donors and raise awareness about their cause. Through powerful storytelling and compelling narratives, Charity: Water taps into the emotions of their audience. They share personal stories about individuals and communities impacted by the lack of clean water, creating empathy and a sense of urgency among viewers. By priming their audience with emotions like compassion and a desire to make a difference, Charity: Water successfully influences individuals to donate and support their cause.

CASE STUDY 3: AMAZON'S PERSONALIZATION AND SOCIAL PROOF

Amazon is known for its highly personalized user experience and effective use of social proof. By leveraging pre-suasion techniques, Amazon has become one of the most successful e-commerce platforms. Through personalized product recommendations based on individual browsing and purchasing history, Amazon directs attention towards items that align with the user's interests and preferences. This personalization creates a sense of relevance and enjoyment, increasing the likelihood of a purchase. Amazon also integrates social proof into the shopping experience by displaying customer reviews, ratings, and "best-seller" badges. By highlighting positive social evaluation and the actions of others, Amazon leverages the principle of social influence to sway consumer behavior. Customers are more likely to trust and make a purchase when they see social proof indicating the popularity and quality of a product.

SUCCESS STORY: BARACK OBAMA'S PRESIDENTIAL CAMPAIGN

Barack Obama's presidential campaign in 2008 is widely recognized as an exceptional example of pre-suasion in political communication. Obama utilized various pre-suasion techniques throughout his campaign to connect with voters and inspire action. Through his speeches and messaging, Obama tapped into the emotions and values of his audience. By framing his campaign as a movement for change and hope, he created a sense of urgency and optimism. He strategically directed attention towards the issues that resonated with voters, emphasizing the need for unity and progress. Furthermore, Obama leveraged the power of social proof by effectively utilizing endorsements and testimonials from influential individuals and organizations. By aligning himself with credible figures and groups, Obama enhanced his credibility and convinced voters that he was the right choice for the presidency. These case studies and success stories highlight the immense potential and impact of pre-suasion. By strategically shaping perceptions, redirecting attention, and leveraging emotions, pre-suasion can significantly influence behavior and persuade others. The key lesson from these examples is that understanding and applying pre-suasion techniques to specific contexts can lead to remarkable results.

Chapter 37: Pre-suasion in Different Industries

In today's competitive business landscape, pre-suasion has become a powerful tool in different industries. By shaping the mindset and perception of their target audience, organizations can effectively communicate their message and influence decision-making processes. This chapter explores how pre-suasion is applied in various industries, showcasing its versatility and effectiveness in achieving persuasive objectives.

1. RETAIL

The retail industry heavily relies on pre-suasion techniques to attract customers and encourage purchases. Using aesthetically pleasing store layouts, captivating window displays, and strategic product placement, retailers can redirect customers' attention towards specific products or promotions. By creating a pleasant and inviting atmosphere, retailers can prime customers for positive shopping experiences and optimize their decision-making processes.

2. AUTOMOTIVE

In the automotive industry, pre-suasion plays a crucial role in influencing consumer preferences and purchase decisions. Through strategic advertising and marketing campaigns, automotive companies can shape perceptions of their vehicles by emphasizing features such as safety, performance, and prestige. Showcasing positive customer testimonials or expert endorsements can also enhance credibility and the overall perception of the brand.

3. HOSPITALITY AND TOURISM

Pre-suasion techniques are widely used in the hospitality and tourism industry to attract and engage potential travelers. By showcasing stunning visuals, highlighting unique experiences, and leveraging social proof, hotel chains, travel agencies, and destinations can create a sense of desire and urgency. Incorporating scarcity and limited-time offers can further enhance pre-suasive messages, encouraging individuals to make bookings or plan trips.

4. HEALTHCARE

Pre-suasion plays an important role in the healthcare industry, both in influencing patient behaviors and healthcare provider decision-making. By framing health-related information in a way that resonates with patients' values and motivations, healthcare professionals can increase compliance with treatment plans, encourage healthier lifestyles, and promote preventive care. In addition, pre-suasive techniques can also be used in pharmaceutical marketing to educate healthcare providers and shape their perceptions of medication effectiveness.

5. FINANCIAL SERVICES

Financial institutions leverage pre-suasion to build trust, establish credibility, and influence consumer behavior. By utilizing social proof through customer testimonials or displaying industry awards, banks and investment firms can instill confidence in their services. Personalization and tailored messaging based on customers' financial goals or life stages can also increase engagement and conversion rates.

6. TECHNOLOGY

In the rapidly evolving technology industry, pre-suasion is essential for product adoption and customer loyalty. By incorporating social proof, leveraging influencers, and using storytelling techniques, tech companies can create emotional connections with their target audience. Emphasizing the benefits and outcomes of using their products or services can further enhance pre-suasive messages and cultivate a sense of urgency.

7. EDUCATION

Pre-suasion techniques are widely employed in the education industry to attract students, engage parents, and influence educational policies. Educational institutions can shape perceptions by highlighting success stories, showcasing alumni achievements, and emphasizing their unique teaching methods. By utilizing social proof and testimonials, schools and universities can build credibility and differentiate themselves in a competitive market.

8. NONPROFIT ORGANIZATIONS

Pre-suasion plays a significant role in the success of nonprofit organizations by influencing public perception and driving donations. By creating emotional connections through storytelling and highlighting the impact of their work, nonprofits can evoke empathy and drive action. Utilizing social proof and showcasing the support from influential individuals or organizations can also enhance credibility and increase donor involvement.

CONCLUSION

Pre-suasion is a versatile tool that can be applied across various industries to shape perceptions, influence decision-making processes, and drive desired outcomes. By understanding the principles and strategies of pre-suasion, organizations can enhance their effectiveness in connecting with their target audience and achieving their persuasive objectives. From retail to education, pre-suasion is a powerful force that can revolutionize the way industries communicate and persuade.

CHAPTER 38: PRE-SUASION AND DECISION-MAKING BIAS

In the world of decision-making, humans are not as rational as we may believe. Our judgments and choices are often influenced by unconscious biases and cognitive shortcuts. These biases can sometimes lead us astray and result in less-than-optimal decisions. However, by understanding and leveraging these biases, we can effectively pre-suade others and guide their decision-making processes. One of the most well-known decision-making biases is confirmation bias. This bias refers to our tendency to seek out information that supports our existing beliefs and ignore or dismiss information that contradicts them. As pre-suaders, we can tap into confirmation bias by presenting information that aligns with the preconceived notions or preferences of our target audience. By doing so, we can reinforce their existing perspectives and increase the likelihood of their agreement. Another important bias to consider is anchoring bias. Anchoring bias occurs when individuals rely too heavily on an initial piece of information when making subsequent judgments or decisions. As pre-suaders, we can leverage anchoring bias by presenting a strong and persuasive initial point that serves as an anchor. This anchor can influence how individuals perceive and evaluate subsequent information, ultimately guiding their decision-making process. The availability heuristic is yet another bias worth exploring in the context of pre-suasion. The availability heuristic essentially means that individuals base their judgments and decisions on the ease with which relevant examples or stories come to mind. To capitalize on this bias, pre-suaders can prime individuals with relevant examples or stories that activate the desired associations or emotions. By doing so, we can influence their perception of the information presented and shape their decision-making process accordingly. Social proof bias is another powerful bias that can significantly impact decision-making. Social proof refers to our tendency to conform to the actions or beliefs of others, especially when we are unsure of what to do. Pre-suaders can leverage this bias by highlighting the actions or beliefs of influential individuals or groups that align with the desired outcome. By doing so, we appeal to individuals' desire for conformity and increase their likelihood of following suit. Recency bias is yet another bias that pre-suaders can utilize to their advantage. Recency bias refers to our tendency to place more emphasis on the most recent information we receive when making decisions. Pre-suaders can strategically present the most compelling and persuasive information right before the moment of decision. By doing so, we can prime individuals to place greater weight on the information presented and increase the likelihood of their agreement. Loss aversion is a bias that pre-suaders can tap into to motivate decision-making. Loss aversion refers to our tendency to strongly prefer avoiding losses over acquiring equivalent gains. By framing the persuasive message in terms of potential losses rather than gains, we can trigger individuals' motivation to take action and increase their likelihood of making the desired decision. Lastly, authority bias is a powerful bias that pre-suaders can leverage in their efforts. Authority bias refers to our tendency to attribute greater credibility and expertise to individuals or institutions with perceived authority. By incorporating endorsements or testimonials from credible sources, we can enhance our own credibility and increase the likelihood of others' agreement or compliance. While understanding and leveraging decision-making biases can be highly effective in pre-suasion, it is crucial to do so ethically and responsibly. Pre-suasion should always aim to positively influence others and guide their decision-making processes without manipulating or coercing them. By aligning with individuals' values, addressing their concerns, and providing relevant and accurate information, we can utilize decision-making biases in a responsible manner. In the next chapter, we will explore the role of attention in pre-suasion and how redirecting attention strategically can enhance the effectiveness of persuasive messages. Stay tuned for Chapter 39: Strategies for Implementing Pre-suasion in Your Life.

Chapter 39: Strategies for Implementing Pre-suasion in Your Life

Implementing pre-suasion techniques in your personal life can greatly enhance your communication skills, influence others more effectively, and achieve your desired outcomes. Whether you want to persuade a loved one, negotiate a favorable outcome, or simply improve your everyday interactions, the strategies outlined in this chapter will empower you to harness the power of pre-suasion in your own life.

UNDERSTANDING THE PRINCIPLES AND STRATEGIES

To effectively implement pre-suasion in your life, it's essential to have a solid understanding of the principles and strategies involved. Start by familiarizing yourself with the key concepts and techniques discussed in previous chapters of this book. This will provide you with a strong foundation to build upon. Once you have a thorough grasp of pre-suasion principles, you can begin to apply them in your daily interactions. Here are some strategies to help you get started:

1. Tailor Your Messages to Align with Values and Motivations

To effectively persuade others, it's important to understand their values, beliefs, and motivations. By tailoring your messages to align with these factors, you can increase the likelihood of their receptiveness. Take the time to listen and observe, and then craft your messages in a way that resonates with the other person's core principles.

2. Utilize Emotion as a Persuasive Tool

Emotions play a significant role in decision-making and can greatly influence our behavior. Leverage this by eliciting specific emotions that align with your persuasive objectives. Whether you want to evoke excitement, empathy, or urgency, choose your words, tone, and body language carefully to tap into the desired emotional response.

3. Establish Trust and Build Rapport

Trust and rapport are essential in any persuasive interaction. People are more likely to be influenced by those they trust and feel connected to. Take the time to build relationships, establish credibility, and nurture a sense of trust. Act with integrity, show empathy, and maintain consistency in your words and actions.

4. Practice Persistence, Adaptability, and Learning from Feedback

Effective persuasion often requires persistence and adaptability. Understand that not all attempts will be immediately successful, and setbacks are opportunities for growth. Learn from feedback, adjust your approach, and continue refining your strategies. Remember that mastery in pre-suasion, like any skill, requires practice and a willingness to learn from both successes and failures.

APPLYING PRE-SUASION IN DIFFERENT AREAS OF YOUR LIFE

Once you have a solid understanding of pre-suasion principles and strategies, you can apply them in various areas of your life. Here are some specific applications to consider:

1. Personal Relationships

In your personal relationships, pre-suasion can help you effectively communicate your desires, needs, and concerns. By tailoring your messages, leveraging emotions, and cultivating trust, you can navigate conflicts, influence decisions, and strengthen the bond between you and your loved ones.

2. Professional Settings

In professional settings, pre-suasion can enhance your leadership abilities, negotiation skills, and overall influence. By using pre-suasion techniques, such as emotional appeals, establishing credibility, and understanding the motivations of others, you can navigate complex situations, persuade colleagues, and achieve desired outcomes.

3. Social Settings

Even in casual social settings, pre-suasion techniques can be applied to make a lasting impression, build connections, and influence others. By capturing attention, providing value, and fostering a positive emotional environment, you can enhance your social interactions and leave a lasting impact.

4. Personal Development

Lastly, implementing pre-suasion techniques in your personal development journey can lead to self-improvement and growth. By persuading yourself to adopt positive habits, overcome challenges, and cultivate a growth mindset, you can achieve personal goals and unleash your full potential.

CONCLUSION

Implementing pre-suasion in your life is a powerful tool for effectively communicating, influencing others, and achieving your desired outcomes. By understanding the principles and strategies, tailoring your messages, leveraging emotions, establishing trust, and applying pre-suasion in various areas of your life, you can enhance your persuasive abilities and create meaningful connections with others. Remember to always use pre-suasion techniques ethically and responsibly, with the best interests of others in mind.

Chapter 40: The Power of Pre-suasion: Final Thoughts and Takeaways

Throughout this book, we have explored the concept of pre-suasion and its immense power in shaping people's perceptions and influencing their decision-making processes. We have delved into the science behind pre-suasion, understanding its frameworks, and exploring the various strategies and techniques that can be applied in different contexts. Now, as we reach the end of our journey, let's recap the key takeaways and final thoughts on the power of pre-suasion. Firstly, pre-suasion is the act of shaping someone's perception or mindset before introducing a persuasive message. By redirecting attention and priming individuals with specific emotions or associations, we can significantly increase the effectiveness of our persuasive efforts. One of the fundamental principles of pre-suasion is understanding the target audience. Knowing their values, motivations, and emotional triggers allows us to tailor our messages and communication strategies to align with their desires and needs. By speaking directly to their interests and concerns, we can capture their attention and build a stronger connection. Emotional appeals play a significant role in pre-suasion. Humans are often driven by their emotions when making decisions, and leveraging these emotions can shape perceptions and guide decision-making processes. By crafting messages that evoke positive or negative emotions, we can influence behavior and increase the likelihood of achieving our persuasive objectives. Additionally, cognitive biases are powerful influencers in decision-making. By understanding these biases, such as confirmation bias, anchoring bias, and availability heuristic, we can strategically leverage them in pre-suasion. By presenting information in a way that reinforces preexisting beliefs, using initial anchors to influence subsequent judgments, and priming individuals with relevant examples or stories, we can guide their decision-making and increase the chances of them aligning with our desired actions or beliefs. Attention is a crucial factor in decision-making, and pre-suasion strategically directs attention towards specific ideas or emotions that align with our persuasive message. By capturing attention through novelty, emotions, and impactful storytelling, we can increase the impact and memorability of our messages. Framing is another essential aspect of pre-suasion. By presenting information in a way that influences perception, we can highlight certain aspects or benefits of our message while downplaying potential concerns or counterarguments. Framing allows us to shape how individuals interpret and respond to our persuasive efforts. Building trust and establishing credibility are vital components of pre-suasion. People are more likely to be swayed by someone they trust and perceive as credible. By being honest, transparent, competent, and empathetic, we can cultivate trust and increase the effectiveness of our persuasive communication. The role of authority in pre-suasion cannot be overlooked. Perceiving someone as an authority figure increases trust and compliance. By highlighting relevant expertise, incorporating endorsements from credible sources, referencing consensus from expert communities, and emphasizing credentials or titles, we can tap into the power of authority and enhance our persuasive efforts. Likability is also crucial in pre-suasion. People are more likely to comply with requests from likable individuals. By establishing common ground, showing empathy, using positive body language, being genuine, listening actively, providing value, and using humor, we can enhance our likability and increase the chances of achieving our persuasive objectives. Setting the stage for pre-suasion is equally important. The physical and social environments significantly influence thoughts, emotions, and behaviors. By designing pre-suasive environments that align with our message, incorporating contextual cues, framing the environment to direct attention, introducing environmental triggers that evoke specific emotions or associations, personalizing the environment, and ensuring consistency between the environment and the message, we can enhance the persuasive impact of our communication. Nonverbal communication is a powerful tool in pre-suasion. Facial expressions, body language, vocal tone, and personal appearance can amplify or contradict verbal messages. By mastering nonverbal cues, such as mirroring and matching, using visual aids, paying attention to microexpressions, controlling gestures, and practicing active listening, we can establish trust, build rapport, and increase our influence in pre-suasion. Storytelling is a compelling pre-suasive tool. Stories engage both the logical and emotional centers of the brain, making them memorable and impactful. By incorporating relevant and relatable characters, conflict and resolution, emotions, and structure, we can evoke emotional responses and create stronger connections with our audience, making our persuasive messages more effective. Pre-suasion is not limited to marketing, sales, or leadership. It can be applied in various aspects of life, including personal relationships, politics, public speaking, and decision-making processes. By understanding and implementing pre-suasion techniques ethically and responsibly, we can positively influence others, build trust, and achieve our persuasive objectives. In conclusion, pre-suasion is a powerful tool that can significantly enhance our communication and influence. By understanding the principles and strategies of pre-suasion, tailoring our messages to the target audience, leveraging emotions and cognitive biases, establishing trust and credibility, and creating compelling narratives, we can increase the likelihood of achieving our persuasive objectives in various contexts. It is important to remember that pre-suasion should always be practiced ethically and responsibly. Respecting autonomy, obtaining informed consent, and avoiding manipulation are essential principles to uphold. By using pre-suasion techniques responsibly, we can make a positive impact and build meaningful connections with others. Thank you for joining me on this journey through the power of pre-suasion. I hope this book has provided valuable insights and strategies that you can apply in your personal and professional life. Remember, the power of pre-suasion lies in its ability to shape perceptions and guide decision-making. Use it wisely and responsibly, and you will become a more effective influencer and communicator.